JOURNEYS

MARVIN WRAY

AuthorHouse™
1663 Liberty Drive
Bloomington, IN 47403
www.authorhouse.com
Phone: 1-800-839-8640

First published by AuthorHouse 12/1/2010

ISBN: 978-1-4520-9971-2 (sc)
ISBN: 978-1-4520-9973-6 (e)
ISBN: 978-1-4520-9972-9 (hc)

Library of Congress Control Number: 2010917331

Printed in the United States of America

This book is printed on acid-free paper.

Acknowledgements

Nothing like this ever happens without the support and sacrifice and encouragement of so many people along the way. I owe a great deal of gratitude to so many people and I know I'm going to send this off and have it printed and realize I've left somebody off that deserved special mention. I apologize in advance.

I am very appreciative of the Northern California Conference for initiating a sabbatical policy that allows pastors the time to engage in some form of study, research project, or just plain renewal. I was privileged to be one of the first to take advantage of it. Unfortunately there was only a minimal amount of funding from the continuing education policy, but I was able to engage friends, church members, and a few other contacts that were willing to invest in a pastor who frequently has very strange ideas.

I am deeply indebted to my church family for giving me not only permission, but also encouragement to undertake this project in the manner in which I did it. I had many sweet "mothers" in the church that prayed daily for my safety. My associate pastors, John Grys and Sherilyn O'Ffill covered the duties at the church and all my terrific lay leaders did what they always do. In addition, my secretary, Sandy Holmes, really held everything together in the office.

Obviously I am appreciative of every pastor and church member I met with along the journey that gave me significant portions of their time and shared their joys, challenges, frustrations, rewards and every other emotion that comes with pastoral ministry.

I am so thankful for James Boyles, a church member, neighbor, but mostly just a great friend who helped me with so many computer technology issues and then read the manuscript not once, but twice and made many helpful suggestions. Mark O'Ffill also offered valuable editorial comments.

Family and friends who prayed for me every day were certainly the ones that really got me through some of the more difficult moments of the journey. I truly felt and absorbed all of those prayers.

What can I possibly say about my one of a kind wife, Ingrid, that would begin to express my appreciation for her patient support? It is certainly not fair to her for me to leave for seven weeks and go on this dream trip while she is left to deal with all of the issues at home. To make matters so much worse she had major foot surgery three days after I left. She has endured so many of my "brilliant" plans through the years and this was probably the granddaddy of them all. But she prayed for and with me every day. She sent along a bundle of cards for me to open along the journey. She always smiled when we were together on Skype and she even left the light on for me when I came home. She has encouraged me as I have labored through the writing of this book and has patiently endured the times when I felt frustrated and pressured because it wasn't getting done fast enough.

So, to all of these and more I express deep thanks, but it is to my sweet wife of almost forty years now that I dedicate this book. She is truly the heart and soul of my life and my spiritual journey and I simply could not have done it without her.

Preface

OK, for one reason or another you have picked up this book. Perhaps you purchased it. Thank you! Perhaps you're just browsing through it a bit to see if you even want to read it. Whatever the case let me just share a brief preface as to what it is all about.

First of all, let me state what will be obvious before long. I am a Seventh-day Adventist Pastor and have been for thirty-seven years. I grew up in the Church of God with headquarters in Anderson, Indiana. However, this book is not unique to Seventh-day Adventist Churches. I believe that the issues involved with church growth and pastoral health would be equally applicable in almost any church. This book is definitely not about Adventist doctrine in any way. Rather, it is about attitudes, flexibility, creativity, openness, and having a true heart to let Christ lead and shine forth in the ministries of our congregations.

I will admit it is a bit late in getting out. I launched the journey on June 8, 2009 and I am writing this preface in July 2010. Mind you, the rest of the book is done, but still that makes well over a year in delaying the sharing of information and the publication process is still going to take several more weeks. The good news, I believe, is that the things I saw and experienced are not fast changing. That also is a mix of good and bad news.

I almost feel that the delay in getting the project completed was God's plan as well. As I write this morning, July 3, 2010 the 59th General Conference Session of the Seventh-day Adventist World Church has just finished and I see many things that can tie into where we may be headed from here.

Please keep in mind that the opinions expressed in this book do not necessarily reflect the opinions of all church leaders, of all my local church leaders, of all my colleagues, or even my lovely wife. In fact, my own opinions are subject to change. And that, my friends, is the hope of the church for the future. Changing needs, methods, and opportunities can influence us. If we refuse to consider change in methodology and even in our theological understanding and application we will cease to be relevant. Make no mistake; I am not talking about doing away with or changing our fundamental beliefs. I am talking about keeping our priorities straight and keeping our eyes firmly on Christ and Christ alone. He is the message. He is the way, the truth and the life.

I think what I really wanted to find out on this journey was what drives the pastors and the church leaders in their ministry. Where is their passion and perhaps the real question is do they have one? What motivates them to continue to worship in their particular church of choice? What are their real and personal core beliefs?

Everyone seems to ask me how I came to choose the particular churches I did. I started with some very specific spots in mind. I definitely wanted to see what was creatively being done in Salt Lake City. I wanted to see what the lasting effects were in Waco, Texas. How do you reach people in a place like Las Vegas? And what do our churches look and operate like in the "Adventist ghettos" like Loma Linda? I knew of some churches that were experimenting with contemporary worship styles and I knew some pastors that I have long admired and wanted to visit with. I also hand picked some churches that I had pastored previously. Finally, there were some churches with just so much history I couldn't miss them, such as Battle Creek.

Other than that, most of the churches were picked somewhat at random to fit a reasonable riding distance for each day. It turned out to be a lot of fun because some of the random choices were the most enlightening. I found nearly all pastors to be interested in the project and not only willing, but anxious to participate. So many were hospitable enough to offer lodging and meals to help cut expenses. I made a lot of great friends and felt a real camaraderie with men and women who are all facing the same great challenge of somehow connecting people with Jesus.

What I found was a pocketful of churches and leaders that seemed to be purpose driven. I found another pocket of churches and leaders that seemed to be struggling to find a common purpose and were often more engaged in debating doctrinal correctness and positioning themselves to "protect" issues, the institution, and personal views. In reality, I believe we need to be presenting Jesus over and over again and allow Him to lead and guide those in whom we are privileged to plant seeds and then allow the Holy Spirit to bring them to fruit bearing followers of Him.

We are not in the business of changing lives. We are not in the business of establishing the personal standards of the person sitting next to us in church. We are not in the business of minutely defining the wording of doctrinal beliefs. We have been called to simply go and make disciples, to preach the gospel, and to prepare people wherever we find them to walk with Jesus through the final days of this earth's history.

We need called and gifted church administrators, but I am weary to death of administrivia. We need a solid organizational structure in our world church, but that structure will never finish the work God has called His church to do. We need policies and principles that bind us together in a church that operates in 200, more or less, countries around the world, but surely we cannot pretend that those policies and principles will be applied exactly the same in every culture. We can't even expect that within the boundaries of a Division as broad as the North American Division.

Let's attempt to be real here my friends. We do have a common calling and goal with every believer from every nation, tongue, and people. We need to gather at the foot of the cross where Jesus' blood flows down to cleanse us from every sin. Having done that we need to take up our cross and follow Him. He is a God of great diversity and He welcomes worship in many forms and practices. His only requirement is that we are truly and humbly worshipping Him and not putting on some kind of performance. It's not about me. It's not about you. It's not about us. It's all about Him. He came. He lived. He loved. He died. He is risen, and He's coming back to take all His children home.

So, I rode nearly 12,000 miles over a period of six weeks and talked to many pastors, and many more church members, and I sought to understand where we are and what we are doing as God's specially called church in these last days.

Intertwined with the reports of those conversations I will share with you some insights into my own personal journey with Jesus. That, too, has been a journey that didn't take the most direct route. But, the journey is not really about the route. It's about the destination.

How about you? Where are you in your own personal journey? What have you learned along the way? Are you closer to the goal that you believe God has for you or are you lost in a storm on some country back road? All I can tell you is that wherever you are, if you cry out for Jesus to be with you, then you are home.

Saddle up friends, it's time to be riding on.

Chapter the First

The First Week

After months of dreaming, planning, preparing and praying, the morning of June 8, 2009 dawned, so full of mixed emotions. I was actually about to leave on a 12,000 mile motorcycle journey all around the U.S. This was a dream of a lifetime. I grew up loving motorcycles ever since my dad would take me for rides on his big old Indian Chief. I raced bikes indoors in Canada and outdoors on flat tracks, enduros, and TT courses in Northwest Washington way back in the 60's and 70's. I had always dreamed of just taking off and riding all over the country, but family and ministry and time just made it seem that would never be a practical idea.

In June of 2008 the Northern California Conference announced a sabbatical opportunity for a few pastors that would submit a plan and purpose. It didn't take me long to initialize my concept. I had, for some time, wished that I could personally visit a wide variety of our churches around the country to see first hand what methods were being used, what passions were being pursued, and whether or not we were really making progress or were we just barely treading water? What, if anything, was really working to reach hearts for Christ?

My project was approved. It was then that I had my revelation. Why not make the journey on my motorcycle? That leads to the rest of the story.

It was very difficult for me to leave Ingrid, my sweet wife, knowing that it would be three weeks before I would see her again. That was made even harder by the realization that she was going to have significant foot surgery two days later, a complication that had come into the picture long after it was possible for me to alter dates, but that fact didn't lessen the anxiety I felt.

She left for her work at the Northern California Conference office where she is the Administrative Secretary to the Treasurer, John Rasmussen. It was easier to have her leave first than it would be to get all my gear on and try to say "good-bye." I still had a lump in my throat. It may seem strange to some, but even though we have been apart due to numerous extended trips throughout our ministry we still find it hard to separate. I think that's a good thing!

Other emotions felt that morning were anxious anticipation and just plain excitement. I had waited for this day through months of preparation and was more than ready to get underway. However, the longest rides undertaken before were several trips up to Seattle and back. Each of those entailed either two or three days of riding each way although I did come back one time with our daughter in one day. That was 850 miles and I've never been anxious to repeat it. The prospect of riding between 11,000 and 12,000 miles over a period of seven weeks was filled with unknown challenges, with weather being a dominant one.

Now the last minute items had to be stored. Obviously there was a lot of time spent thinking and rethinking what to take along. Then I had to decide where to put it and once on the road there were many moments spent trying to remember where I did put it! You might be thinking that there aren't that many options on a motorcycle, but rest assured that with two saddlebags, a trunk, a trunk bag, and a tank bag there are many options especially when you consider the multiple outside compartments on the trunk bag and tank bag.

Finally, everything was aboard and it was now about 8:00 a.m. and time to head toward my first appointment, which was with Dan Appel in Auburn, California. The morning was surprisingly cool for June. We had already had some triple digit temperatures, but now it was quite cool and overcast. The first part of the ride is not particularly interesting heading through Fairfield, Vacaville, Dixon, Davis, and Sacramento, but the sheer excitement of actually being on the way overshadowed the lack of scenery. Dressed in full leathers I was very comfortable and just rolled along while a jumble of thoughts and feelings ran through my mind.

The full itinerary had been set well in advance and I had gone over it so many times. My longest days would be around 550 miles. Today would only be around 470 miles, but there were still many unknowns considering road and weather conditions. Thinking further down the road thoughts surfaced about how accumulated fatigue would factor in. I have a great saddle by Corbin and a gel pad on top of it and that would prove to be important as the trip wore on and my backsides just plain wore. One thing I was not worried about was the dependability of my trusty 1999 Honda Valkyrie. With more than 40,000 miles on the bike already it had never given me a moment's concern. Of course, you never know what can happen, but I can tell you that it performed perfectly for the entire 11,393 miles.

I also had purchased a Dainese full-faced helmet with built in Bluetooth technology. It was difficult to hear when I was going at highway speeds, but remember, I have a six-cylinder engine and six loud pipes coming out the back. It does get noisy! One footnote that should be added here is the great service and help I received from two sources. First of all, Fairfield Cycle, my local Honda dealer, did a fantastic job of servicing the bike and getting it all ready. They even gave me a nice discount! Then there was Cycle Gear. Their shops in Sacramento, Fairfield, and Concord all gave me lots of help and great service as I worked through the trial and error phase of getting equipped. On my second day out the face shield on my helmet broke, but upon arrival the third day in Las Vegas the Cycle Gear manager there fixed it perfectly and it gave me no more trouble the entire trip.

AUBURN, CALIFORNIA

Now, let's get back to the ride. Sailing through Sacramento and arriving at my first destination in Auburn I did experience some challenges in finding the church via Google Maps. I had purchased a GPS device, but found it hard to view clearly, particularly when I placed it under the clear plastic cover of my tank bag for protection from moisture. My second choice was to print out directions, but as anyone who has ever done that you can find that these are not always foolproof. ***One thing I would encourage every church to do is to make sure that visitors can find your facility easily. Large and attractive signs are a valuable asset.*** However, having found the church I must say that Auburn has a beautiful setting and a beautiful facility.

Dan Appel has been in Auburn for just a year and a half. He pastored the Pleasant Hill, California Church for about eight years prior to coming here. I loved sitting and visiting with this big Teddy Bear. It was a good choice for my first visit. I've known Dan for several years and have found him to be warm and creative. In fact he has authored a couple of great books. He wrote "A Bridge Across Time" and, most recently, "The Choice," a commentary for laymen on the book of Revelation.

The Auburn Seventh-Day Adventist Church purposes to be a dynamic church, exalting God in worship, proclaiming His Word, upholding Adventist beliefs, and continuing the ministry of Christ through:

Fellowship with God and one another
Restoration of the love and truth of God
Interceding for God's kingdom to grow
Evangelizing our community for Christ
Nurturing one another to be like Jesus
Discipling others to win hearts to Christ
Serving God as we bless and help others

As we sat and chatted about his first year and a half in Auburn we talked mostly about challenges, perceptions, and misperceptions in pastoral ministry, not necessarily related directly to his current assignment. We've both been in ministry about the same length of time and have seen and experienced many similar challenges and opportunities.

Noting some significant changes he has observed, he talked about the fact that respect for the position of pastor is not a given any longer. This would hold true for churches of any denomination I believe. We have seen too many "celebrity" pastors fall and make headlines.

Additionally the pastor is often expected to be the CEO of the church and for many, if not most, of us that is not really high in our gift mix.

Dan noted another significant change in ministry is that we are finding increasing diversity in our congregations. This diversity is often ethnic, but even more so it is cultural and generational. With longer life expectancies we find ourselves ministering to and leading worship for a wider age range and that can be a big challenge without going to multiple services, which brings its own challenges.

Yet another factor contributing to the lack of assumed trust of pastoral leadership is the fact that within the Seventh-day Adventist Church, particularly, we have created an expectancy of pastoral moves every 3-5 years.

That is changing more recently, but the effect remains. ***How can we expect the church body to simply turn over the function and the vision of the church to the pastor when it will take him or her a year or two just to get to know the congregation and the community and then be moved in another couple of years?***

Throughout my summer's journey many pastors opened up and shared that they were discouraged with the reality of having their creativity and dreams stifled and sometimes even undermined. Having experienced that myself I can openly share that there have been times it nearly took me out of ministry.

In my concluding time with Dan we looked at the bigger picture of the Adventist Church. ***He shared his passion for building relationships first and sharing doctrines once those relationships have been established. The phrase he used was, "We too often make the envelope more important than the letter."*** Dan is involved in Rotary and several other community activities and makes it a point to establish a personal friendship with community leaders.

WINNEMUCCA & ELKO, NEVADA

Now it was time to get back in the saddle and get in some serious travel heading for my evening appointment in Elko, Nevada. Riding east on I-80 out of Auburn you very quickly get into absolutely gorgeous country. I don't particularly enjoy riding on the interstates, but they do, obviously, allow you to gain the greatest distance. However, I-80 from Auburn on into Reno is a very pleasant and scenic ride. You pass through Gold Run, Emigrant Gap, and up over Donner Pass with an elevation of 7,240 feet. The views are just awesome as you roll on through Truckee. In fact, it was difficult to have to roll through, or by, Truckee because it is one of my favorite towns reflecting the old west. But, there were many miles to go before I slept and so I just twisted the throttle and cast a longing eye for my destination and was thankful for no road construction delays on this first day of the journey.

Once you've passed Reno (and I did pass it without stopping for casinos) there's not a lot of scenery to talk about. Everything pretty much flattens out and turns to boredom until you approach Salt Lake City and that wouldn't be until tomorrow afternoon. It was about 285 miles from Auburn to Winnemucca where I stopped to take some pictures of the church. The membership here shows at just over 100, but the attendance averages much lower. It was a pleasant surprise to find the church very attractive both in the building itself and the landscaping. Michael Hope is the pastor of Winnemucca, Elko, and Ely, Nevada and that makes his district 220 miles long. That's a lot of sagebrush to cover!

In Elko Judy Andreson met me at the church as Michael was out of town. Judy is the Head Elder in Elko and she and her husband, Ross, were my hosts for the evening as well. It was so encouraging to find a number of women serving as Head Elders even in areas other than large cities. So often women leaders seem to be able and apt to put more energy, compassion, and intentionality into their leadership. Elko has only about 45 members and about half of that number in average attendance. As in most small, older churches it is hard to find an avenue to growth. There have been some successful ideas tried, however. Judy told me about a "Day Of Singing" that they held at the church some time past. It was simply an afternoon of hymn singing and music with the whole community invited. About fifty visitors came (twice the average attendance at church) and participated and had a great time. They have also done "in home" Bible studies for new women in the church.

Not surprisingly, the same concept came into the conversation that I had with Dan back in Auburn. The real key to having any kind of real

growth and life is in building healthy relationships with the community. Judy expressed a desire to find ways to initiate those relationships and meet the needs of people where they are and to learn about them personally. ***She felt that if she could find six people who would feel called to a similar ministry of fellowship it could make a real difference.*** The spirit in the church is good and they love their pastor. ***It's not the size of the church that matters; it's the size of the heart for God!***

It was a wonderful evening with Judy and Ross and her mother who also lives with them. Ross is a photographer for the local paper and it was such a privilege to see some of his work, which is truly amazing!

In the morning my first big mistake presented itself with the bike. Pulling into their graveled carport, not paying attention to the slope upon arriving, I got up early to leave for Salt Lake City and found that there was no way to get enough traction on the gravel to push the 740 pound bike back into the alley. I tried for quite some time before finally giving up and going in to wake up Judy and ask her to move the car so I could maneuver the bike around and get on my way. Lesson number one: check your exit before you enter!

SALT LAKE CITY, UTAH

Leaving Elko, the next destination was the Wasatch Hills Church on the east side of Salt Lake City to meet with leaders there. It was not long before the clouds encroaching on my horizon began to cause a bit of anxiety and noting that their color was starting to match the color of my bike, which is black! You can see great distances ahead because if you think Nevada is flat then western Utah would have to be compared to a tabletop. I thought often about the movie, "World's Fastest Indian," which featured Anthony Hopkins as Burt Munro, the New Zealander who in 1967 set a land speed record with his 1920 Indian motorcycle. That is one of my all time favorite movies. I resisted the temptation to stray off of the pavement passing the Bonneville Salt Flats to see what a 1999 Valkyrie could do. Other than watching the salt flats there wasn't much to do except dream and watch the darkening sky. The sprinkles did start, but didn't develop enough to cause me to put on rain gear. It must also be noted that as you approach the city of Salt Lake the scenery once again becomes very impressive. Just east of here are some fantastic ski areas that we have enjoyed in the past.

I arrived at the Wasatch Hills Church, on the east side of Salt Lake City, in the early afternoon and found a great team of church leaders and a wonderful lunch waiting for me. What a delight that was! There to meet me was Bernie Anderson, the Sr. Pastor. Also present was the Youth Pastor, Darryl Priester; the Secretary, Carol Allison; an elder and Worship Committee Chair, Carlos Linares; and the Head Elder, Karen Bray, another woman Elder and a very competent one at that. She really has some energetic plans. I was surprised when Karen asked me if I had ever been in Clearlake Highlands, CA. I had been a Student Pastor there 36 years previously. She had been a teenager in that church and we had the privilege of having dinner in their home on a few occasions. Obviously the assumption must be made that I hadn't changed much over the years and that was why she was able to recognize me.

I was particularly interested in finding out what kind of outreach might be effective for an Adventist church in the headquarters of Mormonism. The Wasatch Hills Church has a membership of about 340 and is a healthy church. They have been in existence about 50 years and have a high percentage of professionals. ***I found the key to their health being that they were willing to think creatively and endeavor to reach people where they are. Again the concept of building relationships first came to the surface and I was not the one to bring it up.***

They have a program called ICOR (Inner City OutReach), which targets the needs of residents who are not getting all of their needs met by social service agencies. They go beyond just supplying food and clothing and actually try to reach into the hearts and minds of those that they serve.

Another very creative outreach that would not find approval in every congregation is called "Brewed Awakenings." The subtitle reads: "Real People, Real Questions, Real Coffee." Nobody is trying to change the health emphasis here, but they are meeting the people where they are. I found that an attitude similar to this was present in almost every church that was vibrant and growing. I also believe that this fits the New Testament model.

Pr. Bernie is a member of the Chamber of Commerce and he also takes advantage of where they live by bringing in celebrity speakers such as members of the Utah Jazz NBA team and was even able to get Tony Dungy, former Head Coach of Tampa Bay and Indianapolis NFL teams to come and speak. ***Efforts like this may not instill our distinctive doctrines, but they sure can bring people into contact with the church and begin to build a relationship.***

My feeling as I left this fellowship was one of warmth and joy. This was a place where I felt cared about and affirmed. I'm not saying I didn't feel that in the other places throughout my sabbatical, but it was very tangible here. ***The emphasis of this church was on belonging first and believing as a result.*** Most of the staff came out and wanted their picture taken on the bike before I left and that was pretty fun too.

TIRES

I began moving south now and hugging the western edge of the Rockies. The clouds were looking very angry, but at times it seemed that a Divine map maker was able to change the direction of the highway just in time to avoid the moisture that they surely held in store.

My destination now was just north of Price, Utah to a little town, aptly named Helper. According to Wikipedia, Helper is situated at the mouth of Price Canyon, alongside the Price River, on the eastern side of the Wasatch Plateau in Central Utah. Trains traveling westward from the Price side to the Salt Lake City side of the plateau required additional "helper" engines in order to make the steep (2.4% grade) 15 mile climb up Price Canyon to the town of Soldier Summit. Helper was named after these helper engines, which the Denver and Rio Grande Western Railroad stationed in the city. It was there that I had an appointment with Carbon Emery Motorsports to get a new set of tires. Obviously I had a few thousand miles already on my current set and I didn't want to take any chances as I was heading through country where there would be some uncertain country roads.

Last year I had the "privilege" of experiencing a blowout at 80 mph. I was fortunate that it was the rear tire, but I can assure you it still causes a great deal of internal excitement! I was on I-680 in California at the time and I had all the cars slowing down and moving to the shoulders as I took up all the freeway lanes just trying to stay upright, which I did. However, I have no desire to repeat that experience. You may now be wondering why this good preacher man would be doing 80 mph. All I can say is that it's California, baby! I was trying to avoid getting run over by all the 85-90 mph traffic!

I only get around 9,000 miles out of a set of tires and they cost around $700 by the time you get them installed. My installation always costs more because you have to remove the saddlebags and the six exhaust pipes. It always takes longer, too, because those pipes are hot, hot, hot when I come in. The mechanics at Carbon Emery did a great job and three hours later I was ready to go, but it was too late to go very far so I just rode a few miles down the highway to Price.

The ride that afternoon down Highway 6 was gorgeous, gently curving, and rich with sights to please the eye. It became evident that I didn't dare observe the scenery too closely, however, because I came upon mule deer on several occasions and they don't know about jaywalking being illegal. Mule deer are nearly as large as elk and there were more than a few on the side of the road sleeping until Jesus comes. I did not want to add to that number and certainly didn't want to join them!

BRYCE CANYON AND ZION NATIONAL PARKS, UTAH

After a good night's rest in a local motel I was ready for a great ride through Bryce Canyon and Zion National Parks. It is a beautiful ride down Highway 10 until it intersects with I-70. Thankfully, I had been tipped by one of the mechanics the day before about a frontage road that offered much more beauty than the Interstate. It didn't even show on the atlas, but it was a wonderful ride with virtually no traffic and lots of sweeping curves to add to the scenic beauty. I picked up Highway 24 in Sigurd, Utah and rode that until it intersected with Highway 12 in Torrey.

Today was the first time I actually put on the rain gear and, amazingly, the only time on my whole east bound journey. Today also marked the highest point in elevation on the entire trip passing a sign on Highway 24 noting the elevation at 9,975 feet. The showers were not interfering with my joy one bit as I viewed a constantly changing landscape of alpine meadows.

Following Highway 12 proved to be delightful and finally I arrived in Bryce Canyon National Park. One of the delights of being in your 60's is that you qualify for a Senior Pass to all the National Parks. It costs just $10 for a lifetime pass. Now that's a good deal since it would otherwise cost me $25 for each entry and there were going to be four of them on the trip. At the Park Entrance I asked the ranger about the best scenic spots as my time was unfortunately limited. At Bryce you don't have to go far to see spectacular formations. Just a few miles into the park you can view some of the most beautiful views imaginable. I went to Bryce Point and then worked my way back with stops at Inspiration Point, Sunset Point, Sunrise Point, and Fairyland Point. Every stop was awesome!

The disadvantage of my planned itinerary was that it didn't allow for a lot of time for just enjoying the beauty of the land. Appointments had been made well in advance and I was just trying to get an overview of some areas I not seen before so I would know where to bring my wife on a future trip. This is a must!

Back onto Highway 12, I rode until it connects with Highway 89 and headed toward Hurricane, UT, which was my destination for the night. Only about 350 miles would be covered today, but considering the stops and the country roads it was going to be a full day. When you're on Highway 89 heading toward Hurricane and St. George you don't have a choice about visiting Zion National Park and you wouldn't have a choice about whether or not to pay your entrance fee, but I don't think anyone ever complains. In the San Francisco Bay Area you pay up to $6 just to cross a bridge every day and other than the Golden Gate Bridge there isn't all that much to look at. I flashed my Senior Pass once again and was allowed into spectacular formations that were a constant delight on either side of the highway.

The beautiful scenery didn't stop beyond the boundaries of the park either. There was plenty of beauty to distract me from watching the road, but I did pay attention and made several picture stops. All in all it was a wonderful day with only a few light showers and the new tires were a great mental comfort.

ST. GEORGE AND CEDAR CITY, UTAH

Once in Hurricane, and checked into my motel, I called the St. George and Cedar City Pastor, Bob Maehre, and found that he actually lives in Hurricane. Meeting him at his house the next morning I learned that Bob has been there for about three years and when he came neither church had a building of their own. The Cedar City Church has grown in that three year period from 26 members to 76, and most of that growth represents new converts! They get many interests from 3ABN (Three Angels Broadcasting Network) and ***he attributes their success to the welcoming and loving spirit of the church.*** They recently purchased a building from a Jehovah's Witness congregation and have added classrooms and a fellowship hall.

The St. George congregation has a higher percentage of professionals and has only existed in St. George for the past seven years. Prior to that the congregation was in La Verkin and I understand that the transition had some challenges. The membership shows 126 and approximately 80 attend regularly, which is higher than the average. Bob kept talking about their new building. He told me they had purchased a barn and were remodeling it. I kept getting a mental picture of a barn for a church and the picture was not necessarily exciting.

I followed Bob to the new location and was exceedingly surprised and impressed. First of all, the location is in a very upscale new residential area. The "barn" was indeed built for that purpose, but you have to see it to understand. This was part of a larger property that went into foreclosure. The home next door is amazing and has an actual water park in the back yard complete with waterfall and slides to rival Six Flags! The barn itself is virtually new and the remodeling consists mainly of partitioning rooms for classes and getting the main area ready to be a sanctuary. It is going to be absolutely lovely! This indeed was not a barn. This was a beautiful building that God has reserved to be a beacon for truth in a challenging environment.

We went on into downtown St. George to see the storefront they are currently renting from another congregation. This is going to be an enormous improvement for them and should enhance their growth prospects greatly. Of course, this is still Mormon country and visitors will pass many of their churches. Near the new Adventist church site I saw two large identical Mormon churches with only a driveway separating them. I asked Bob about this and he said that when a church gets full they just build another one even if it is right next-door. You can imagine how challenging it must be to make converts in this kind of environment.

We also stopped at the local temple and found it interesting to note that the front door had no latch on the outside. You have to be let in. I watched as a young boy walked up the steps and looked for a way to enter the facility. He looked so disappointed to find that he could not go in. ***Unfortunately I have seen some other churches that may as well have been built that way. We need to make it easy for people to find their way into our churches. We need to open the doors for any and all who would desire to enter in.***

LAS VEGAS, NEVADA

It was a delightful visit with Bob, but now I needed to make my way to Las Vegas to meet with Denny Krause at the Mountain View Church. There is a dramatic scenery change involved here. The change is from interesting rock formations to "interesting" billboards! As you approach the city of Las Vegas you become bombarded with signage that is highly animated. Everything moves and is designed to catch your eye. Is it any wonder, therefore, to discover that the fastest growing church in Las Vegas is extremely high tech? This is a graphics driven city.

The Mountain View Church is definitely a growing church. Current membership runs about 950+ and attendance on any given Sabbath is something over 500. It was a really fun hour and a half sitting and talking with Denny Krause, the Sr. Pastor. ***As we began to chat he shared that he feels the biggest drawback to church growth is that we fail to recognize the needs of the people we are given to serve.*** We need to constantly be evaluating what we need to do to attract secular minds and keep them interested. ***Denny has every new member fill out a questionnaire to find out what brought them to the church and what is keeping them there.***

So, I asked him, "Where do the people come from that come to your church?" His answer amazed me. He said that they baptize between 30 and 40 people every year whose first contact is through Three Angels Broadcasting Network (3ABN). I had to ask him how in the world that was happening. 3ABN is a pretty conservative format and would not seem to naturally lead someone to a high tech, very contemporary worship style.

He explained that when an individual finds 3ABN and has not already

had much, if any, contact with the Seventh-day Adventist Church they are neither conservative nor liberal. They may not even know what those terms mean in a worship context. They simply want to learn about the Bible. They will watch the programming for a year or so and then will often look in the phone book to see if there is an SDA church near them. Being the largest church in Las Vegas, Mountain View has the largest ad and people will come to check it out. And Mountain View is ready for them!

On an initial visit the newcomers will receive a brochure, a book, and a five-dollar gas card. The card has a note attached that says, "We want you back and we'll pay the gas." Denny said they spend around $300 per month for this offer. On the second visit they will receive additional material, but no more gas cards. ***By the time they have attended four worship services the guests are connected to a small group and within two months they are placed in a ministry group. The result is that they tend to stay and become involved.*** As they make close personal contacts and are actually allowed to be a part of ministry even before they consider membership they know that they are truly considered as part of the body of Christ!

Denny felt strongly that the factors that are key to their growth and to keeping new members are:

1. Contemporary music
2. General attitude of acceptance
3. Casual dress
4. Not majoring in minors
5. A wide variety of classes and groups that meet real current needs

He also felt that to a large degree the church has lost its mission emphasis on the local front. We have become too project oriented rather than people oriented. This seemed to tie in with what Dan Appel had shared earlier regarding how we have made the envelope more important than the letter.

A question Denny is always asking is, "If the church disappeared, would anyone notice or care. With that in mind the Mountain View

Church partners with the local elementary school and makes the neighborhood surrounding the church and school their number one focus. They don't try to reach the whole of Las Vegas, but they want their neighbors to see them as a vital part of the community.

BARSTOW, CALIFORNIA

Originally I had planned to stay in Las Vegas with Denny, but their family plans took a last minute change and so I elected to head south a bit and get out of Las Vegas. They say, "What happens in Vegas stays in Vegas" and I didn't want to happen there! Leaving in time to be just ahead of the heavy traffic on I-15, I was happy to get some more miles done. Once you leave Las Vegas there aren't a lot of great stops heading south, but I decided to take advantage of the cheap rates offered by some of the casinos. So, bear with me now, I stopped in Primm, Nevada and checked in at Whiskey Pete's Casino. Now, you might think that's a pretty strange place for a Seventh-day Adventist Pastor to pick, but at $29 for a large non smoking room far away from the casino noise I'd say it was good stewardship!

The next morning I loaded up and rode down I-15 to Barstow to meet with Richard Parent. Richard has an interesting background and was fascinating to talk to, having pastored for 21 years in Canada and then six years overseas as a Mission President and a theology professor. He has been at Barstow for three years.

Barstow's unique opportunities come from being very close to two military bases. The interests and members that come from these sources are, of course, temporary, but it has provided some great opportunities for talent and for outreach. Barstow also gets a lot of truckers and tourists and they have found a weekly "mini-potluck" to be quite successful.

Perhaps the most unique and valuable outreach is related to Richard's opportunity to teach at the local community college where he teaches classes in Contemporary Religions, Introduction to the Bible, Bible as Literature, and Ethics. While he can't teach SDA doctrine there, it does open up many opportunities to share his faith and to foster continuing discussions and relationships.

Some of the challenges they face in Barstow are related to the fact that Loma Linda no longer administers the local hospital. That change took place twelve years ago and as a result of families moving away they no longer have a school open.

The local membership is well aware of the challenges. More local leaders are getting involved with both working and brainstorming and Richard is very hopeful that things will turn more positive as they focus on a reclaiming project this fall.

LOMA LINDA, AZURE HILLS, CA

In the early afternoon I rode down to the Loma Linda area. It's an interesting ride down I-15 leaving the desert behind and coming into San Bernardino. It was a great surprise, however, to encounter rain. It was not enough to warrant the rain gear packed in my bag, but enough to make me think about it and to watch the curves a bit more carefully.

It was a great privilege to stay Friday night with Darold and Carol Ann Retzer. This was a wonderful change from the motels I had stayed in for the past few nights. Darold and Carol Ann are friends of ours and he was the Conference President in Northern California when I came to Napa. He is now the Executive Pastor at the Loma Linda University Church, which has a membership larger than many conferences. We had a delightful time sitting and chatting for a couple of hours about the challenges of a church that size.

Obviously they are going to have resources that most other churches don't have, but reaching the people and meeting their needs present the same challenges. The Loma Linda Church does some traditional evangelism, but one of their main outreach tools is their TV ministry, which goes worldwide.

This brings up an interesting point related to how people connect with churches today. In Napa we also have a TV ministry, but it only goes to two communities. A local cable company provides this and at first I thought it would have limited value. However, I have been amazed at the number of people that stop me in stores or on the street because they recognize me and they tell me that they often watch our services. Our cost is minimal although we have spent some significant dollars as we have upgraded equipment. To start, though, you can get by with a pretty simple approach and it is amazing how many people watch local programming.

Another tool related to this is live streaming on the Internet and archived sermons on the website. We have received emails from people all over the country as well as from England, Scotland, Germany, and Russia who watch our services. This, also, is not expensive and does provide significant outreach. I will add that website appearance, ease of navigation, and keeping everything current is a vital aspect of having it be a truly useful tool. We need help with this in our own website in Napa. ***Most church websites I visited as I tracked down information related to my visits were standardized and offered very little in the way of relevant information other than a contact number for the pastor.*** We live in the times of technology folks. We need to be in the game and I know that I need to find someone to help us right at home.

OK, let's get back to Loma Linda. ***Darold shared with me that they have a very heavy emphasis on children's, youth and young adult ministries.*** Again, they are going to have multiple resources available, but ***the point is that this needs to be a priority target in every church if we expect to stay alive and current. It takes time and it takes money, but there is no more significant investment that a church can make.***

One unique idea came into the conversation. During the winter they have a five-week series called "Winter Wednesdays" and they provide a supper and seminars. This has been quite popular and allows a relaxed time of fellowship and spiritual food along with the physical food. This is another fairly simple concept that most churches could accomplish.

On Friday afternoon I met with Daniel Belonio, pastor of the Loma Linda Filipino Church, for a great lunch and then went to speak at his church for Friday evening vespers. The Filipino congregations are always fun to worship with and it's really hard to find warmer fellowship.

They have a great congregation and I would say their key attraction to growth is simply their love. That really is the bottom line to any church's growth and outreach isn't it? They do it very well here.

Daniel is a fellow biker and plans to do a similar research project to mine and visit Filipino congregations around the country to see what is happening. I wish you well, Daniel. Get a good seat pad!

On Sabbath morning I decided to check out the CrossWalk fellowship in Azure Hills. I had heard about this venture that was spawned from the Azure Hills Church and wanted to see what was happening in a fairly new intentionally crafted contemporary outreach.

I will say that I did have a difficult time finding the place. It is located in a very nice rented space in a large business complex, but the only signage I could find was on the front of the building and I couldn't see that from the side streets. I was there for the early service and so it took awhile before I saw some people gathering and figured that this might be the place.

Once inside I was free to wander about, pick up a program/information sheet and look around. I'm fine with that, but ***I was a bit surprised that I was not engaged by anyone until the "meet and greet" part of the service.*** I was certainly not trying to avoid being approached. I was doing my very best to look like the visitor/seeker that I was. No response. ***Likewise, afterward I meandered around for a full fifteen minutes, but was not approached by any members.*** I wore my bike clothing of long sleeved shirt, jeans (complete with chain secured wallet) and boots. I thought I would look like I belonged there. Maybe I looked too in touch. ***Dear friends, from every church, if you see someone you don't know it is your privilege, calling, and responsibility to connect with them. This is true of every member in the church. That connection may well make an eternal difference!***

I will say that the service was great. They have good music that is well presented and Michael Knecht, the Lead Pastor, gave a great message. The entire wall behind him on the large platform is a screen with very effective visuals. ***One part of the service that I particularly enjoyed was a prayer focused on one family that had gone through several significant trials recently. That was a very powerful and touching moment in the worship experience.*** I had a great time, but if someone was seeking and was a bit insecure they might be missed.

So, I hopped on the bike and did get a few admiring looks as I let the sweet noise roll out of my six exhaust pipes. By the way, I did have to wipe the water off of the seat and windshield as the skies continued to provide a light drizzle. This seemed strange for southern California at this time of year. Once I got back into the high desert above San Bernardino the skies were once again clear and I stopped to take off my leather jacket as things warmed up quickly.

You meet all kinds of people and drivers on the highways. Not all of them are fans of motorcycles either. Riding on I-15 back toward Barstow, in order to pick up I-40 and head east toward Kingman, AZ and then the area south of the Grand Canyon, I found myself being tailgated by a younger woman in a BMW. Now, when I'm riding on the highway I will pretty consistently do about 5 – 8 miles over the posted limit and will keep with traffic. I don't want to stand out, but I just want to flow with the majority. I also like to ride with plenty of clear space ahead of me. I usually describe my riding style as cautiously offensive, rather than defensive. I want to be the one making the decisions and not left trying to react to someone else's choices. When I am following someone it's hard to see objects in the road that a car might pass over, but could cause a challenge to a two-wheeler. A relatively small chunk of truck tire can be a big problem. This driver was no more than ten feet behind me and I was pretty uncomfortable. I was keeping up with the car ahead and we were slowly, but consistently passing cars to our right. Finally I just looked back and put my hand out with a stop gesture and she just backed right off and, in fact, dropped so far back I never saw her again. I don't know what she was thinking, but I didn't want to find out either. I was blessed my entire trip with no real close calls and no notice from Highway Patrols.

KINGMAN, ARIZONA

Now headed east on I-40 it was smooth sailing for a great Sabbath afternoon ride of 280 miles to Kingman, Arizona. It was certainly very warm going across the Mojave, but it wasn't terribly uncomfortable. Wearing a long sleeved shirt and occasionally stopping to spray it with water makes hot weather riding much easier. The church in Kingman is located well on the outskirts of town and is located high on a hill. ***I was pleased to see that they have a huge sign that is easily seen from anywhere***

near the area. The Arizona pastors were all at campmeeting and I was going to be with them in Prescott, AZ on Monday and hoped to meet with as many area pastors as possible. I did learn that they had just done an evangelistic series with Scott Hakes that resulted in 13 baptisms and 3 Professions of Faith. Kingman's unique outreach is to the privately run prison and the Mojave County Jail. The whole area has a huge methamphetamine problem and several members from the church work diligently to reach out to individuals and families impacted by this. ***This is yet another example of meeting the needs unique to your local area. Other churches should not seek to copy this ministry necessarily, but should seek to determine what the people in their community need most.***

Pastor Jack Robinson also informed me that the church had recently been remodeled. ***I found throughout my journey that the condition and décor of the church and the property tells me a lot about the spirit and outlook of the congregation. It is true that we can worship God anywhere, but keeping the church clean and up to date makes a huge impression on first time visitors.***

Originally my plans were to stay in Kingman, but I decided to push on another 125 miles to Williams, which is at the base of the road leading up to the Grand Canyon. The thought of spending two nights in the same room was too much to resist. In addition I wanted to get up to the Grand Canyon early and get some sunrise pictures.

GRAND CANYON, AZ

On Sunday morning I started out early, having set my alarm for 4:00, and jumped on the bike in the dark to head up to the Canyon, which was about 60 miles away. It got very cold heading upward in elevation. Keep in mind that the Canyon is at 7,000+ feet. The overnight temperature was 33! I especially paid attention to the signs for deer and elk crossing and then I saw the one that said to watch for mountain lions for the next 10 miles! That certainly took away any urge to make any side of the road pit stops! The sun started coming up when I was still a few miles from the park. Soon it was obvious that I should have started out 30 minutes earlier to catch the really red skies, but it was still beautiful. The scenes took on a very unique look, as there were some significant forest fires in the area and parts of the canyon were filled with heavy smoke, which made for some unusually spectacular photos.

You can easily spend several hours just moving from viewpoint to viewpoint. Each one offers a unique perspective of the beauty below. As the day progresses the shadows change as well. I was only able to visit the South Rim, but it was a wonderful day. It was as much fun photographing birds and wildlife as it was taking pictures of the Canyon itself. I also met a lot of interesting people from a wide variety of countries and parts of the USA. Being on the motorcycle provided an opportunity for easy conversations as many people were interested in where I was from and I was also able to share the purpose of my journey. I met many men who were jealous of my being able to take a seven week bike trip and still call it work!

On my way down from the Grand Canyon I rode through Flagstaff to get some pictures of the church there. David Hakes is the pastor and ***the church is fairly small, but absolutely delightful. It occupies a corner in a great neighborhood and is very attractive with beautiful landscaping. It made a truly inviting visual appeal!*** I was sorry that I didn't get to connect with David at campmeeting the following Monday, but I'm sure some very positive things are happening there.

How delightful it was to return to Williams and not have to unload all the gear! I needed this rest from the travels I had experienced. This now marked the completion of my first full week. I covered just over 2,200 miles and saw a lot of country. I was beginning to feel comfortable with my routine and was already excited about many of the contacts I had made and observations that were coming together.

I can say right here that every pastor I talked to over the entire trip was serious about their ministry. Every one of them wanted to work hard and serve God well. ***However, I could already begin to see (and I will have more to say about this later) that many congregations are not willing to let their pastor lead. This is especially true in the smaller and mid-sized churches. It is also too often true that conference leadership is hesitant to encourage real creativity. Far too often numbers and dollars drive us. We are slow to value and embrace uniqueness in our outreach and we are also very slow to allow significant and meaningful change.***

I want desperately for this book to maintain a positive outlook and reflection. I do not want to be critical of any church, the denomination as a whole, or its leadership. Those in top leadership positions face challenges that local pastors cannot fully appreciate. They also have to answer to their own constituencies and are forced to consider where their support comes from, but, at the same time, I do have to be honest to what I have seen and what I perceive after 37 years of ministry in various capacities. When you look back at what has transpired over the past 165 years it is nothing short of a miracle. ***We, by God's grace and power and Divine leading, have done amazing things, but in today's fast changing world we have to find ways to stay current in technology and methodology without throwing away the heart of our message.*** This is going to be a major battle and we may well find more opposition from within than from without.

So, week one covered 2,200+ miles through four states and connections with 10 pastors representing 14 congregations. I was surprisingly refreshed and still excited about the journey ahead. I had been blessed with good weather and safe travels and fellowship that foretold of heaven. How thankful I am for modern technology! Thanks to an abundance of Internet connectivity options and free Skyping I was able to talk to and see my sweet wife almost every night of the trip. That was also true when I was in Mozambique for three weeks earlier in the year building a church with a group of our members. It was still hard to be away from her for that long, but Skype made it a whole lot easier.

Chapter the Second

The First Decade

Life began for me in Seattle, Washington in the Greenwood Maternity Hospital. As you might expect, if you know me, I made quite an entrance. Somehow the umbilical cord managed to wrap around my neck not once, not twice, but three times! By the time the birthing process was complete I was literally blue and that oxygen deprivation may explain a lot about me today!

After two weeks my mom was able to take me home to Edmonds, just sixteen miles north of Seattle and right on the shores of Puget Sound. Growing up there as a boy, I never truly appreciated the amazing beauty of that place, but I sure enjoy going back now. A particular love of mine is the ferry ride from Edmonds to Kingston where many days you can see Mt. Rainier and Mt. Baker among the Cascades and also the Olympic Range on the Peninsula. As a young boy I loved those crossings to Kingston, Bremerton, and Vashon Island to see relatives. The love is still there!

I don't remember a lot about my actual birth, as I was quite young at the time. I do know that as a few years passed I tended to see my world as a lot bigger than it really was. That was made clear when my sister shared a couple of pictures showing the "living room" of the first house in my memory bank. There was barely room for a small sofa, one chair, a coffee table and a piano. My parents, my sister, and I all shared one bedroom and, of course, one bathroom. The only other room was the kitchen, which also had the table and chairs for meals.

From what I understand this house was an upgrade from previous houses. My mind is filled with a bounty of fond memories from my pre-school years on through about age 9. I also remember my dad's Indian Chief motorcycle and the rides we took with me hanging on to his leather jacket. That is undoubtedly where I got my first love for motorcycles. We also went to a lot of motorcycle hill climbs and those are hard to find today, but they were about the most exciting thing I could think of. The sounds of roaring engines, the smells of the rich oil and gas mixture, and the sights of the colorful helmets and jackets are all still clear in my mind.

Picture, if you can, a hill approximately 400 feet high and very, very steep with ruts and always at least one terraced section. Most riders never made it to the top and many flipped over backward in the effort. Helpers from the side would immediately rush out and attach ropes to the bike to keep it from rolling and crashing down the hill. I can remember several riders being taken off by ambulance to treat injuries and one spectator, as well, that was hit by a rock shot out from the chained rear tire. My, oh my, but that was exciting stuff!

Looking back it appears that we would have been classified as poor, although I didn't realize it. I know we ate a lot of horsemeat because it was cheaper than beef. That was not all that uncommon at the time. We also raised rabbits in the large field out back and I remember having to help kill and skin them. We had a big cherry tree and a large section of raspberries as well as a good sized garden. Best of all we had a whole block of forest separating the three neighbor boys and us, one of whom was my age. There simply isn't enough time or space to begin to tell you all of the escapades we dreamed up. Some I can't tell you because I'm not sure the statute of limitations is up yet! We spent most of our time climbing trees and having "wars" in the forest, playing baseball, and fishing for trout in the stream that ran through the neighbor's property. How proudly I returned home with my prize catch and asked mom to "slaughter my fish."

These were the summer days when you were allowed to go and

play when breakfast was over and any chores were done and you didn't have to come home until dinner unless you wanted some lunch. One bright day our enterprising minds were hard at work and we decided to make some quick cash by digging and selling worms. We knew that the local hardware store sold them for bait and we dug a whole wagonload packed in nice rich soil. Proudly we pulled the wagon the half-mile into town and offered our wares. Imagine our disappointment when the owner told us he already had enough inventory of worms. We felt very hurt and put out by this turn of events and decided that we needed to make a statement. So we took the wagon out on the sidewalk and emptied the whole load right there and then ran home. For the next few days I trembled every time the phone rang, sure it would be the police reporting my crime. Actually the hardware store owner probably just scooped them up and added them to his stock for free.

Another ingenious idea was conceived all by myself. It was Mother's Day and I wanted to give my mom a flower, but had no money. That didn't deter me, knowing that a nearby neighbor had a yard full of them. Being too shy to go and ask Mrs. Kunz for a flower, I decided to use stealth tactics. We had an old empty chicken coop out back and so, for whatever reason beyond my ability to recall, I decided to crawl under it and then under the fence separating our yard from Mr. Dalby's. Then staying low to the ground I crawled behind his vegetable garden and into Mrs. Kunz's beautiful flower garden. Picking a beautiful bouquet of carnations (I love the smell of carnations!) and retracing my route, I finally presented my wonderful gift to mom.

Something about my appearance, and perhaps my smell, tipped her off and she began to ask embarrassing questions. This resulted in my being ordered to appear at Mrs. Kunz's front door with an explanation and an apology. This was a very painful experience for a pre-schooler and I wish I had learned my lesson well here, but it was to be repeated on a grander scale in the next decade. So, there I was facing Mrs. Kunz, who was a very sweet and loving lady. She took one look at this quite disheveled little boy with a pathetic looking cluster of flowers in hand and figured it out. I apologized with tears and, bless her heart, she gave me a hug. Then she told me that I could come and pick all the flowers my heart desired if I would only come to the door and ask permission. She next proceeded to make a lovely bouquet and even placed it in a vase for me to take home to mom. That was a lesson in grace that has stayed with me all through the years.

My sister, Phyllis, was four years older and how I envied her getting on that big yellow school bus every morning as the bus stopped right at the end of our driveway. The year before my entrance to Kindergarten I begged mom every morning to be able to wait at the bus stop with the big kids. She was always hesitant to allow this because the highway ran in front of the house and traffic went by pretty fast. Finally one day I somehow succeeded in gaining her permission, but there were rules. First, there was to be no running and second, I was not allowed to go past the ditch that ran between the highway and the tall hedge.

All went well until the game of tag broke out. To start with I stayed back out of the way, but then Jimmy started right for me and I would be "it." There was simply no choice. It was run or be "it". I ran down the narrow strip between the hedge and the ditch, but then there was another hedge that cut off my escape and so the only option was to jump over the ditch…right into the highway…and right into the path of a dual oil tanker coming downhill at about 50 mph. Frozen in my tracks with eyes tightly closed, the sound of the air horn and screeching tires filling my ears, I waited for the impact. Obviously, since I am writing this today, the driver was able somehow to miss me and when I opened my eyes the truck had skidded past me and was no more than a foot from my side.

The next few moments were somewhat of a blur. I remember the truck driver coming at me with a very red face and yelling and me thinking, "You really shouldn't be yelling at me mister." Then I heard the sound of footsteps running. My mom was running! My mom weighed over 200 pounds and was only 5'-2". I don't remember her running any other time in my entire life! But, she was running and surely she was coming to rescue me from that mean truck driver. Well, she scooped me up in her arms and began to kiss me, which was quite embarrassing, and then she took me behind the hedge, pulled down my pants, and proceeded to spank me. Mothers are very confused people! I still have the letter that she received from the oil company thanking her for her letter of commendation and the $25 gift for the driver, which was a pretty hefty amount for those days. I know I will recognize my guardian angel. He, or she, will be the one with the greyest hair and the most haggard expression.

I could go on for pages telling you stories of my early childhood and most of them would be true! It wasn't a bad time at all, but I began to learn at an early age that my relationship with my dad was going to be tricky. My 5th birthday is very clear in my mind. I don't remember what presents were received, but I remember my dad coming to me and sticking out his hand. He said, "You're five years old now. From now on we don't hug. We shake hands like men. Don't call me daddy. My name is Rolly. You can call me Rolly." It would be over fifty years before I ever hugged my dad again.

Through the following years he told me many times, "I made two mistakes in my life; first there was your sister, and then there was you." Another favorite comment of his was, "I hate all kids, but I hate mine more than any of the others." My dad was good to us in many ways. We went camping every year and to the Western Washington State Fair in Puyallup, but he almost never played with me. As a teenager he would play horseshoes with me, but that was about it. He was a man to be respected and feared. If I kept my distance everything was fine, but when there was disobedience the punishments were sometimes harsh, but not actually abusive. Looking back in later years the thing that hurt the most was that there simply was no relationship. Any time of his that I took seemed to be more of an inconvenience for the most part. I don't recall thinking about it very much as a boy. It just became second nature to stay out of his way.

The beginning of my school years was a delight to me. School was great (except for the first day of Kindergarten that I spent crying) because there were other kids to play and associate with. Other than our neighbors I was never allowed to go to other houses and was never allowed to bring friends home. I learned early to entertain myself with games, but school gave me dozens of close friends.

It is probably safe to say that I've always been somewhat of an extrovert. That was probably to get the attention that I sought at home from Rolly, but never got. I have a report card from second grade that gives this written comment from the teacher: "Marvie is a good student, but he talks too much." My wife will tell you that things haven't changed all that much through the years.

It was while I was in second grade that my parents decided to try to move to either Los Angeles or Phoenix to find better work. Rolly was an auto mechanic and he wasn't finding satisfactory work in Seattle at the time. I remember many parts of that experience that lasted about three months before we returned to Edmonds. Still fresh in my mind, is the memory of stopping at the Christian Brothers Winery in St. Helena, California (the building is now the Culinary Institute of America) and being able to go into the wine tasting area, put my foot up on the rail and get a sarsaparilla. Rolly, of course, was sampling the wine and that was the first time I recall realizing that he was beginning to drink a lot. I didn't think about it much at that time, but it would play a significant role in the future years.

I also remember going to Knott's Berry Farm. Trust me, it wasn't anything like it is today, but it was still very exciting to a seven year old boy. I'll never forget going on a train ride and a bunch of outlaws stopped the train and came through the cars threatening to rob all the people. That was scary, but it sure was fun! There was also this cool guy in a jail cell who knew my name and a lot about where I was from and all that. How did he know all about me? (It's OK, I know now.)

Back in Edmonds, after unsuccessful job searches, school resumed in the 2nd grade at Edmonds Elementary. Interestingly, on my sabbatical trip this year I revisited the building, which is now an adult education center, and was able to walk back into that same second grade room. What a flood of memories came back visiting that and other rooms where I sat as a boy. It's amazing how comfortably strange it feels to go back in time for a few moments. It has been 57 years since I was in second grade, but it felt like I was right back there. I want to thank those who helped me with editorial suggestions for holding back on the temptation to make comments on that one!

The elementary grades passed with relative ease and school continued to be a haven for me. I can remember every teacher that taught me and each of their names and I have no doubt that those who are still alive remember me as well. I was never a "bad" kid, but I sure tried their patience with my antics.

In the summer between fourth and fifth grade we moved to a bigger house. I would miss my neighbor friends, but I was excited because there was going to be my very own bedroom. It was out in the garage, but that was fine with me as it provided even more privacy. I built a crystal radio set and would listen to the Seattle Rainiers of the Pacific Coast League play baseball long after I was supposed to be asleep. I loved that room and the opportunity of being alone.

It was mentioned earlier that I became very adept at making up games to play by myself. Some of these were quite intricate. I would take six dice and every possible configuration of numbers would be assigned a baseball play. I made up a league of eight teams and had them play a series of games against each other to see the league champion over the course of a summer. I also would play outside with a ball, bat and glove and would hit the ball straight up, high into the air, drop the bat, grab the glove and catch the ball. If I missed that was a hit for the other team. I got quite good at that. I do believe it caused me to pop out a lot in real baseball!

So ended the first decade of my life. That summer I turned two digits old! That was a big thing for me. Now as I'm fast approaching three digits it's not nearly as exciting to mark the advancement of time. Let's get back to the ride and we'll pick up this journey in chapter four.

Chapter the Third

The Second Week

ARIZONA CAMPMEETING, PRESCOTT, AZ

On Monday morning I packed things up and headed to Prescott, Arizona to check in at the Arizona Campmeeting and sit down with some of the Arizona pastors. It had been so nice to have two nights in the same motel. There wouldn't be an opportunity to have that privilege again until the end of my eastbound ride when I would be in Virginia and with family. It was a sunny and gorgeous day for riding and I had to start out by backtracking about 20 miles to pick up Hwy. 89 South. Unless you've experienced it you can't fully appreciate what it is like riding through the pine forests and on the bike you get the full benefit of the smell of the sun on those needles. I was riding though a lot of the Prescott National Forest and enjoying every minute of it. Well, at least I was enjoying it until I read a sign that said, "Highway Flushed With Oil Next 12 Miles." Oh, I just love riding my bike on freshly oil-flushed highways. It saves on getting your lube jobs! Actually it didn't turn out too bad as the work had been done the previous week, but it is those kinds of signs that can strike fear in the heart of a motorcyclist.

Camp Yavapines is a truly beautiful location and facility. However, in finding it I was reminded that you can't always trust computerized directions. Following the instructions exactly placed me sixteen miles away from where I needed to be. Oh, it was on Iron Springs Rd for sure, but it was also in the middle of nowhere. Fortunately there was a little store with a very helpful and accommodating woman who let me use the rest room (first things first!) and then let me use her phone, as my cell phone had zero reception there. Eventually we got it all figured out and I was on my way. Perhaps not all accidents are bad, as it did result in a great conversation with the owner of the store and she was genuinely interested in my project and had many questions about the Seventh-day Adventist Church. Maybe the directions were divinely inspired after all. Maybe, just maybe GPS stands for "God's Preferred Sequence!"

Arriving at Camp Yavapines and parked in the parking area it was interesting to see, as I first walked on the grounds, a tent with three nice cruisers parked underneath. I made that my first stop and I met Shannon and Justine who represented the Sabbath Keepers' Motorcycle Ministry. Their group was based in the Kingman, Arizona Church, but the ministry has chapters in many churches throughout the western states. The national headquarters is in Hollister, CA. I would certainly encourage you to check it out online if you have any interest in being a part of a ministry that involves motorcycles. Shannon is a deacon in the Kingman Church as well and was very helpful in getting me some of the information regarding their ministry, as Pr. Jack Robinson was busy with duties. The extra good news was that they let me bring my bike in and park it in the shade and out of the dust!

One of the great blessings of campmeetings is the number of friends you can run into. I found Ralph and Darlys Robertson, which was absolutely delightful. Ralph was the Ministerial Director here in Northern California for several years and it is always so much fun to connect with "old" friends.

I was also happy to see Frances Wightman. Frances was a member in the Napa Church and still returns each year during tax season, as she is a CPA. When it was time to leave the campground I stopped by her Fountain of Youth Salon and Day Spa. What a wonderful setup she has there along with her son, Lonnie. We had a wonderful lunch in a Mexican restaurant and she sent along a nice bag packed with an orange, apple, peach, nuts, and banana bread. Not a bad deal huh?

So many of the pastors I wanted to speak to were busily involved with responsibilities and could not break away. I did get to spend an hour with John Martin, however, pastor at Holbrook Indian School. We talked about his ministry to and through the kids at this unique school. ***He spends a great deal of time with them just building connections. They baptized 16 last year plus three Professions of Faith and they have baptized 15 already this year.***

We talked at length about the uniqueness of his church and it's setting on the Indian reservation. ***But as he talked I sensed a very real and sincere passion that he had grown to have for these kids. He told me about one young lady who was struggling with her decision during a baptismal service. Afterward he talked to her and asked if she wanted to be baptized. She said she did and then she went outside and talked two of her friends into being baptized as well. As he shared that story his eyes filled with tears and his love for the kids was clear.***

Obviously this is a key ingredient for successful church growth. I have found that if the people know that you truly love them things will happen. I think this is mostly because they will feel safe in inviting their friends to come with them. Love and acceptance are far more important than technology and programming. It's not going to be enough to say you are a loving church. You are going to have to demonstrate it consistently to everyone who comes through your doors.

I have to add a sad note to this portion of my journey. As I am doing the final editing, nearly a year later, I have just learned that John collapsed at the campmeeting in 2010 and died just a few days later. ***This gentle, loving pastor will surely be missed by all who knew him and especially by the members and students at Holbrook.***

John was the only pastor I was able to find in the time frame set in my crowded schedule. I would love to have been able to spend more time here in Prescott as well as in many of the other places I visited, but I had set a fairly rigid itinerary for myself. Maybe next time: Ooops, I promised Ingrid there wouldn't be a next time.

HOLBROOK, ARIZONA

Now it was time to head east again and stop at the Holbrook Mission School that Pr. John Martin had told me so much about. I rode along Hwy 169, a beautiful winding road, and then picked up I-17 back up to Flagstaff and then east on I-40 to Holbrook in order to save time. Time was constantly one of my nemeses on this journey. Everything always was about the schedule it seemed. There were so many side roads I would love to have explored and interesting places to just spend time with and so many people who had nothing to do with the church work that would have been fascinating to talk to, but that was not the purpose of the sabbatical.

Holbrook Indian School was pretty quiet upon arrival and most of the staff and crew were gone for the summer. There was some work going on, however, and I ran into Steve Alred and a group of students from the Sacramento Central Church. They were doing a mission project down there and had been working hard renovating the dorms. What a delightful surprise to find friends so far from home!

I found the whole campus, which covers some 300 acres, to be very clean and inviting. The school is for boarding students only and John Martin has built some very strong relationships with the young people. ***I am continually reminded on my journey that relationships are really what it is all about isn't it?***

After a very comfortable night at a Comfort Inn I hit the road pretty early. There were two major challenges that I would be facing today. First I would lose an hour once I hit New Mexico. This had been delayed since Arizona does not have Daylight Savings Time. That also meant that I would lose another hour tomorrow. When you're running on a tight schedule this doesn't help.

My second challenge today was going to be the temperatures, which were predicted to be in the high 90's and low 100's. It is about 240 miles from Holbrook to Albuquerque, but my route would keep me on I-40 and there's not much to stop you. The scenery is not what I would call breath taking, but it does get interesting in places. Shortly after starting out you ride through the Petrified Forest National Park and I certainly did see some unique rock formations right along the interstate. It's really easy to get hypnotized when you ride long distances on very straight highways in the heat with little or nothing to break the monotony. The biggest thing to watch out for is the pieces of truck tires that lie scattered on the road. You certainly don't want to follow one of those 18-wheelers very closely. Not only can they blow a retread, but they will also pass over the remnants without swerving and that leaves you very vulnerable. Many thanks be to God that I didn't connect with any pieces of significant size throughout my journeys.

ALBUQUERQUE, NEW MEXICO

By the time Albuquerque came into view it was definitely warming up and I was glad to pull into the parking lot of the Albuquerque Heights Church on Wyoming Blvd. NE. I could see two things immediately. First, this was a beautiful church, and second, they were in the midst of a very major renovation both inside and out.

Unfortunately, the pastor, Hector Quinones, had just had back surgery and I was not able to visit with him directly, but a good sense of what was happening here was shared as I visited with the church secretary, Lorraine Peek. Bless her heart, she was working faithfully in the midst of building chaos, but she certainly had things under control. Just a few minutes with her made me feel like I was talking to a long time friend.

This brings out a key point in reaching new people. Our churches need to be easy to find and attractive to the eye and then it is critical that the

individuals they meet on first contact, either in person or on the phone, are welcoming, informed, and loving. In the case of the Heights Church, it was obvious that things were in disarray, but it was also obvious that this church had a plan and was on the move. Even the construction workers that I encountered were helpful and fun to talk to. When I got to Lorraine's workplace I was immediately put at ease and she shared her time willingly with me.

Lorraine described the church as very conservative, but very loving. ***I am convinced that it is not the worship style that determines the growth factor. It is the love style that makes the difference. If the emphasis of the church is on the needs of those who come and the emphasis comes from the heart it really won't matter all that much whether your worship is contemporary or traditional. People may have a personal preference for one style over another, but genuine love will outweigh that preference every time.***

At the Heights Church they have been active with evangelism in the traditional setting. Most recently they had a series with Jack Colon. ***The youth are very active in visitation to a variety of homes for children as well as the pediatric unit in the local hospital. This has been a very effective outreach to families.*** Once again I found that a number of interests have been garnered from 3ABN. Lorraine described Pr. Quinones as energetic, charismatic, and real. She attributed the latter description to his background in the Catholic Church and struggles he faced as a youth. Like the good loyal secretary she was she did not elaborate on the latter.

Walking away from this visit I knew that I had been in a place that was healthy and focused on their ministry. They were caring for and investing in their facility. The current two-phased project will cost about three million dollars, but will result in a beautiful place of worship that includes a gymnasium. They are in a prominent location and are taking advantage of it fully. ***Albuquerque Heights Church is certainly a good resource for ideas for many churches that prefer to stay with a more traditional worship format and outreach methodology.*** This, and other churches, can be easily found on the Internet. Some have very helpful websites.

One last side note is that Lorraine is the aunt of Chris Oberg, now Sr. Pastor at the La Sierra University Church. She obviously has some close ties to effective ministry.

After spending an hour and a half here I needed to get down the road another 210 miles to Roswell in order to meet with church leaders there that evening. These distances in wide open country are not all that difficult, but the temperatures can really eat into your energy reserves and on those long straight stretches of state highways you can not only lose your focus, but can actually get sleepy! On three or four occasions I found myself wanting to nod off and that is not a good thing with any vehicle, but is particularly frightening on a bike. Frequently I made myself stop and take some pictures, whether there was anything worthy of the effort or not. I would stop and get a drink, but often it was a long distance between places to purchase such a thing. I would sometimes sing to myself, and wearing the full-face helmet that was pretty interesting. Actually I found the full-face helmet to be cooler than the shorty helmet I also had along. Sun protection also became a major issue. Anything exposed turned red pretty quickly, so I was wearing long sleeved shirts and gloves, but had a hard time keeping the wrist area covered and so I relied on generous portions of sunblock. With all the precautions and effort I still managed to get some interesting color spots!

I rode east on I-40 for about 60 miles and then turned south on Hwy 285. Some stretches covered more than 14 miles without a hint of a turn. I would play games by picking out a point ahead and guessing the distance, and was almost always short on my guess! Most of the time on these stretches my speed was averaging about 80 mph. The speed limit was usually 70, but I figured that first of all, I was not likely to find a speed trap on these more remote highways, and I also assumed they would cut you some slack. On some of the portions of interstate I found speed limits as high as 80. You could make some really good time there!

About an hour north of Roswell I was really looking forward to checking into a good motel and taking a cool shower before my meeting with the group from the Roswell Church. It was really hot with temperatures well over 100 and when you have that heat, plus the heat reflecting back up from the highway, plus the heat from the bike engine it gets a bit uncomfortable. Some people have the notion that the wind keeps you cool. Unfortunately I think the wind operates more like a convection oven!

While dreaming of my cool shower, a car doing between 110 and 120 passed by. All I know for certain is that he was nearly flying by me. About a half hour later I caught up with him as traffic was stopped and a helicopter was landing on the highway. I was able to move to the front of the line, but the highway was completely closed. The car that had gone by me earlier was clearly in view. It was well off the road and had been modified considerably by rolling multiple times. We waited in the blistering sun for over an hour with no shade available. Some wonderful people invited me to sit in their car with them finally and that certainly saved my day. I learned later that the driver did not survive. It was a sobering reminder of the consequences of taking too many risks. Pulling into Roswell I passed the 3,000-mile mark and said a prayer of thanks to God for safety!

ROSWELL, NEW MEXICO

Even though it was late getting into Roswell I opted to get my room and take that shower first. I called Tom Jordon, the Head Elder, and arranged to make our meeting a bit later and I think we were both glad for that as I not only looked better and felt better, but undoubtedly smelled better as well.

This is an interesting town to say the least. It is famous, of course, for its "alien" sightings and some of the stores going through town reflect that "fame." I was surprised to see the size of Roswell, which boasts a population of about 50,000. Riding through the length of downtown I didn't see any beings that looked suspicious, but suspect that some of them may have been checking me out.

It was nearly dark when I arrived at the church and got together with Tom Jordon along with Daniel, Debbie, and Alyssa Ramirez. ***The Ramirez family is fairly new to the Seventh-day Adventist faith and they have not wasted any time in getting involved! The pastor, Ken Davis, lives two hours away and has a three church district spread over 200 miles. In these scenarios if the church is going to grow at all it is going to have to come at the hands of the local members.***

I saw a couple of quite unique, but wonderful, ideas in Roswell. The first thing I noticed as I walked inside the sanctuary was that there were posters on the walls everywhere. In fact, there were sixty-six of them! Each one represented a book of the Bible and as people completed reading that book they could sign their name to the poster. ***I can't imagine that a lot of churches would want to decorate their sanctuary this way, but it certainly was a fun and positive way to encourage Bible reading and generate congregational participation.***

The highlight of my visit with these local leaders was when they asked me if I would like to see their Prayer Ministry. Of course my answer was, "Yes." They took me outside and led me toward a building in the parking lot that I had assumed was for storage. Well, I was very wrong.

Stepping inside you will find a nicely prepared waiting room. A participant begins with an orientation as to what they will experience and a church leader first prays with them and then asks that they remove

their shoes as they prepare to move into Holy Ground. Passing through a curtain the participant comes to the first station, which provides a basin, and asks that they wash their hands and a reading explains the cleansing power of God. Each station is separated from the other to provide privacy and enough time is allowed so that no one needs to feel rushed. At the second station they kneel to pray over their needs and write them on a piece of paper and then attach the note to a brick with some putty and carry it with them. At the third station they write a particular focus of their burden in a tray of sand, pray over it and then smooth the sand. Next they pray at a table with a large chain depicting the binding effect of sin and it's burdens. The next station depicts the chain broken and they take a piece of broken chain with them as a reminder of God's power and they also leave their brick with it's attached burden. They next can place a marker on an area locally, statewide, nationwide, or worldwide depicting a prayer need and finally they have a chance to journal. They report that most people spend about an hour and almost nobody comes out with dry eyes.

I was tremendously impressed with the quality of the environment they had created, but I was even more impressed with the quality of their hearts as they shared this ministry and their vision for it. They have a desire to make this available 24/7 so that anyone with a breaking heart can come and pray with someone who will guide them. This was one of the most creative ideas I saw on my journey.

After the long rides, the heat, the accident witnessed, and the inspiring visit I was more than tired and was very glad to get back to my room and crash. Another challenge to this mission was that no matter how tired I was there was the need to make notes. From the beginning of the journey, and in fact for months in advance, I had kept a blog going so those from my church, my contacts along the way, and any others who were interested could keep up to date. There was also the need to reconnect with the pastors and churches to be visited on following days, and last, but never least, Skype with my precious, patient wife. There was also the daily challenge to unload and reload the bike, and check the directions for my next stop. As much fun and as exciting as this sabbatical was, it was still a lot of work and I was always thankful for a day that allowed a little less travel and a little more reflection time.

CARLSBAD, NEW MEXICO

Thankfully, I only had a 75-mile ride the next morning from Roswell to Carlsbad and a chance to meet Erwin de Graaff. It's funny how with certain names you sometimes get an idea of that person's appearance before you meet them and then sometimes you get really surprised. This was the case with Erwin. I was anticipating a Dutch background, and was somewhat correct, but it was Dutch New Guinea, so I was met by an Asian face! We had a good laugh over that. Erwin is such a delightful pastor and he showed me around their steel frame building, which was very nice inside. I actually found quite of few of these structures in this part of the country and they seem to work very well and are much less expensive to construct.

This is Erwin's first pastorate as he comes from a teaching background. He was born in Indonesia and moved to the Netherlands at age six and to Pennsylvania at age thirty. He met his wife in Alaska and they have three children and she home-schools them.

Carlsbad is a struggling town. The only real attraction there is the Caverns and the town has a large turnover and therefore so does the church. Many of the professionals have left and it is a challenge to infuse confidence and vision and motivation into the members who are left. They do a lot of evangelism and health outreach, but find it hard to get commitment from the community. This is the type of church and district that is common across much of America and it is a challenge to enable churches to grow and sometimes even to just hang on. God bless the pastors and lay leaders who endeavor to do God's work in regions that are difficult to live in, let alone build churches.

To add to the challenge, Erwin also has responsibility for the Roswell Spanish, Saragosa Bi-lingual, and Van Horn Spanish Churches…and he doesn't speak Spanish! ***Can I solicit a prayer for Erwin and his family and the multitude of other pastors and their families that have similar challenges?***

I mentioned to Erwin the prayer ministry seen in Roswell and he asked if I would like to see theirs as well. He took me into a side room and showed me all the same stations set up in a similar fashion to what I had seen the night before, but I sensed that it was not fully the same. He then told me that they were seriously looking at taking this down and turning the room back into Sabbath School rooms. The difference? ***No one in Carlsbad had the burning passion for that particular ministry. That is not a negative statement regarding Carlsbad. No one ministry or outreach opportunity is right for every church, but whatever method of outreach is used there has to be an individual or a group that is passionate about it.***

My next stop was Abilene, Texas, and that was 325 miles away and it was already hot. Between Carlsbad and Abilene I can't say much about the scenery because there really wasn't much to say anything about! The most interesting thing I saw was a Roadrunner that barely made it across the road without me hitting it. I kept my eye out for Wylie Coyote too, but he never showed. This afternoon was simply one of survival. I stopped a little more often to just stand in an air-conditioned convenience store and drink an electrolyte type drink and get my body temperature back down a bit. As with yesterday the dream of a cool shower kept me moving down the highway and I was thankful for the 80 mph speed limit, which I fudged on just a wee bit.

ABILENE, TEXAS

An interesting experience presented itself at the front desk of the Comfort Inn in Abilene. That motel is on the same frontage road as the church and I asked the young desk clerk which direction the church was. She said, "Oh, are you a Seventh-day Adventist?" I replied in the affirmative and then she said, "So, you don't eat pork or shell fish and you don't smoke or drink!" I just smiled and said, "Is that all you know about Seventh-day Adventists? You are definitely missing the best parts." She told me that she was studying with some members along with her mother and they had just gotten to the study on health. I parted with the comment, "Just keep studying, but remember that Jesus needs to be your focus and He has you covered, no matter what!"

I had not been able to connect with the Abilene pastor, David McLaughlin, but I saw in the phone book that they had Wednesday Night Prayer Meeting and so I just showed up. I later found out that I had written down the email address incorrectly. It's always interesting to see the various expressions when I ride up to a church that isn't expecting me. We're not usually sure how to react to someone who doesn't meet our "normal" expectations. The group in Abilene was very welcoming and gracious and it was a delight to join them in their mid-week worship. David presented his continuing study, but was kind in allowing me the opportunity to share the purpose of my journey and to encourage his group in their outreach endeavors.

The building is another steel structure, but even so it has left the congregation with a burdensome mortgage. Abilene was typical of so many of the churches I saw across America that struggle to maintain an attractive facility, to effectively reach new interests, and to fully engage the younger generations. They are doing a great job here, but it is difficult and I wonder what many of these groups will look like twenty years from now.

I did consistently find groups of people that were loving, willing to talk, and eager to listen, but I sensed that real creative changes directed to younger adults were going to be hard to sell. This was not just the case here in Abilene, but many places I visited gave me the same feeling. It was about here that I began to coin the phrase, ***"Pockets of Hope,"*** related to the overall health of our church. ***I had already seen so many churches that were just "getting by" but I couldn't see a lot of hope for real significant growth. This is not the fault of the pastoral leadership and I'm not laying the responsibility at the feet of the lay leadership either. In fact, I'm not blaming anyone, but I strongly feel that our conference leaders need to openly encourage, reward, and facilitate creativity. We need to be well read regarding what is happening all around us in the thinking of young adults. We don't need to change or soften our message, but we need to seriously evaluate our methodology.***

As we continue to look at new methods I think we need to recognize how quickly trends and thinking changes in today's world. It may be more than difficult to stay up to date with architecture, worship style, and all of the technology, but we desperately need to be aware and open to what is going on outside of our church walls. ***One thing is never out of date. Genuine love and acceptance is always in vogue. If we couple that***

with a willingness to give our youth and young adults the opportunity and space to share their gifts in worship I believe we will see positive results.

On Thursday, June 18, I had a chance to catch up just a bit. The ride from Abilene to Waco is just less than 200 miles and after about 50 miles of that on I-20 I was able to leave the interstate and get on State Hwy 6, which took me serenely into Waco.

WACO, TEXAS

It was surprising to see the size of this town, which is really quite beautiful and is the home to Baylor University. Reaching my motel for the evening with time to spare I was thankful to find a new washing machine and dryer available and was even able to iron three shirts, but I hope Ingrid doesn't read this part of the book! There were also several phone calls to confirm connections over the next week and time needed to make sure of the routes to be taken.

It is amazing how much work is involved in making contact with 70 pastors and working out a schedule that makes all of this possible. There is such a wonderful camaraderie among our pastors and lay leaders alike. I have been welcomed into their homes and have been blessed by them willing to share their time and their hearts with me.

Feeling refreshed and ready now I went to take some pictures of the Waco Church. The Head Elder would not be able to meet with me until tomorrow morning, but the pictures needed to be taken today. The church is in a good location right along the highway and makes a very nice presentation to people passing by. Of particular notice, as you first approach the church, they have a whole section of parking spaces near the main entry designated for visitors as well as some for handicap parking. That appearance and effort to make visitors feel valued and welcome are very important factors in those opportunities for first impressions. ***We need to engage people before they ever get in the door.***

It was very good to get a good night's rest and have a travel bag full of clean clothes again. I rode across town on Friday morning to meet with Kraig Turpin, the Head Elder of the Waco Church. Kraig is the office manager for a medical practice and was a delight to talk with about the past and the future of the Waco Church.

Waco was one of the churches specifically picked out to visit. I wanted to see how a church responds when national attention of a negative sort is placed on it. I'm sure we all recall the news coverage of the Branch Davidians and David Koresh back in February of 1993 at the Mt. Carmel Center just outside of Waco. It's hard to imagine that has been some eighteen years ago and yet Kraig assured me that the impact was still being felt in the Waco Church.

In addition to the challenges that come with such memories Waco has had a continuing strong infiltration of Shepherd's Rod and Davidian believers. There have been times of so much disruption and division that the church had to close its doors for several months and meet in homes. They have also had to obtain restraining orders at times. Interestingly these more extreme groups believe that Waco is the "New Jerusalem" due to its being the exact opposite on the globe to Jerusalem. They may need to consult their globes a bit more carefully and take notice of the equator. ***Can you imagine what an impact this kind of disruption and division would have on any attempts to positive outreach with a true gospel message? Kraig estimated the average age in the church to be about 65. There are 70 – 80 in attendance with only 8–10 youth.*** They were in the midst of a pastoral change at the time of my visit as well.

However, there are certainly bright spots and beams of hope as Waco looks to the future. Kraig was indeed optimistic and positive about possibilities. They have a very active and effective community service program that offers help with clothing, food, finances and even medical help. They also have a very active prison ministry and have more than 200 Bible studies going with inmates across Texas.

Certainly the Waco Church and its leaders need many prayers to be able to move beyond their past and reach out to new young families in this beautiful city. ***There is no room for those whose aim is to divide and disrupt. I don't know what all the answers need to look like, but I do know that only Christ's spirit of love, compassion, patience and understanding will meet the needs of new young families. Sometimes we need to make a complete break with the past in order to move on.*** Pray for Kraig and his fellow leaders as they seek to make a new story for Waco.

IRVING & JOSHUA, TEXAS

Now I'm off to Irving, Texas, which is just outside of Dallas and only a little over 100 miles. What a nice treat to have such a short ride and arrive in the early afternoon at the home of Tony and Mary Morales, who graciously opened their hearts to me. I had met them when they visited our church in Napa. They found out about my upcoming venture and asked me to stay with them and go to church with them. Having not finalized on a church in the Dallas area I accepted their warm invitation. What a delightful Sabbath it was indeed! Fellowship with true Christians is always easy and always sweet. To make things even sweeter, Tony is a biker! I'll say a bit more about that shortly.

After a delightful afternoon and evening of visiting and sharing and a night of peaceful sleep I went with them (in their car!) to their "Cowboy Church" in Joshua, Texas. The church name is "Crossroad Fellowship", but the portrayal on the front of the church shows a horse standing and a cowboy kneeling before a cross lets you know that this is indeed a cowboy church. This was one of the most delightful Sabbaths of my life. Pr. Henry Reid is just one big smile and that smile is reflected on the faces of all the members I met. They are just one welcoming and loving entity. ***The fellowship meal after church was fantastic and you had the feeling that this was a family reunion more than a church gathering. I think that is what it is supposed to be like isn't it?***

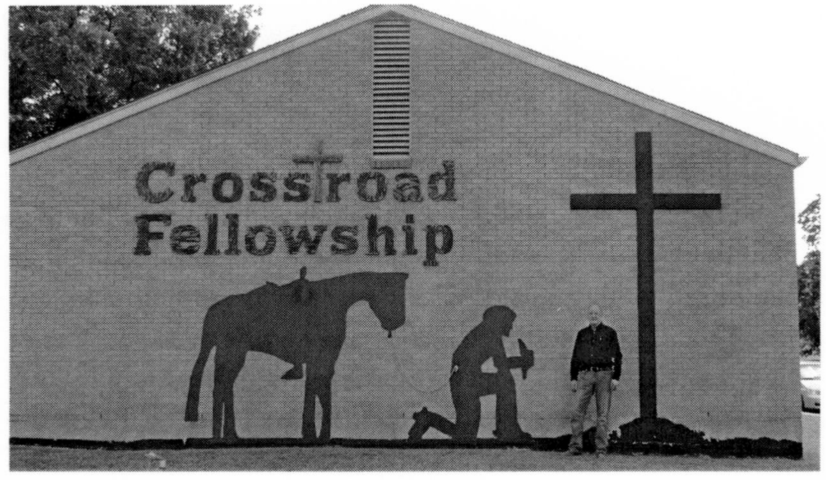

This is just one more illustration that the key to doing Christ's work as a body is not about a building and it's not about a worship style. It's not about technology and it's not about how we dress. It is about the joy of salvation, the love of God, and a passion for people. Who cares whether you are in a church of 50 or 5,000 if you're made to feel welcome and loved? I would say the Crossroad Fellowship Church had a little over 100 in attendance that Sabbath. They will probably never grow to be a mega church, but they have a mega message of love and a church full of people with stories of conversion. I'd go back there any time.

I rode back with Tony and Mary, changed clothes and hopped back on the bike and Tony did the same as he rode with me for quite a while. We stopped for gas and for him to turn back and he noticed a plastic cover on my air vent that was broken. He had the answer in a short belt that held it tight. I want you to know, Tony, that the belt is still doing a fine job! We separated with a prayer and a hug and I was on my way to DeKalb, Texas to stay with Reg and Betty Phillips.

There was one little mishap as I got near to my destination. Stopping for gas in DeKalb, the bike was in a somewhat awkward position as I filled it without getting off. I put the debit card in my shirt pocket and in this heat was not wearing any jacket. So, motoring down the highway to the Phillips' home I saw something fly by my eyes. It was my debit card and it was gone! Upon reaching my destination I called Ingrid and she arranged to cancel that card and she would get a new one and bring it to me when she flew out to join me in Virginia. Seems like she did have something to say about my being more careful. What a delightful wife I have! She has bailed me out more than once!

DEKALB, TEXAS

Reg Phillips is the pastor of a two church district in the Texarkana area. For Reg this is pretty much coming home as he grew up in the area and has built a lovely home on family property next to his mom and a brother. This was wonderful country living and Betty fixed a fantastic southern hospitality meal, which I greatly enjoyed. Reg and I had a fun visit just talking about his two churches that are trying to deal with all of the normal challenges found in smaller to medium sized churches.

It is always difficult to find enough committed leadership to effectively reach new families and individuals and it is also challenging to gather adequate funding for innovative projects. Most of these kinds of churches have long histories and change and adaptations don't come easily. For pastors with multiple churches it is often enough of a challenge just to meet the needs of existing members and then try to provide ministry opportunities that will work in their surroundings. Reg and Betty are of good courage, but the challenges are daunting. I had a great night's sleep and a marvelous breakfast to start me on my way. Today would be a very big challenge with a ride of well over 500 miles and temps expected to hit very near 100.

Sunday was just plain hard work in many respects. I did put in 510 miles and it was very hot. The highest reading seen on any signs was 99, but it sure felt worse than that. The morning hours were, obviously, not as bad heading east into Texarkana and then south toward Shreveport. Beginning the day in Texas I would go through part of Arkansas and then across Louisiana, Mississippi, and on well into Alabama. It would have been so much fun to take a more leisurely pace and visit with people along the way, but I was again finding myself racing against the clock to meet an evening appointment.

I didn't take any pictures of that day's travels and just kept riding along and looking forward to the gas tank getting below the ¼ full mark so I could stop. I even fudged a couple of times and stopped earlier just to cool off and drink, but every time it took another fifteen minutes off the clock and a pastoral couple in Tuscaloosa, AL was waiting for me. Every time I stopped there was also a phone call to Ingrid just to hear her voice and keep her up to date on my progress and to let her know I was fine. I was also anxious to hear about how her foot was doing after the intense surgery she had just after my exodus. Those moments on the phone were more refreshing than the drinks in many ways.

TUSCALOOSA, ALABAMA/COLUMBUS, MISSISSIPPI

Finally, my Google Map directions led me to the apartment of Jon and Libna Arroyo, the pastoral couple for Tuscaloosa, AL, and Columbus, MS. Once again we are dealing with two small to medium size churches, miles apart, with very unique needs, opportunities, and challenges.

This couple was so delightful. They are young and full of the joy of ministry. I caught them at a very awkward time in their journey as they had just learned that they were being transferred to Bass Memorial Academy. Their two-bedroom apartment was full of boxes and they were nearly ready to move. I sincerely offered to stay in a motel, but they would not hear of it and I was destined for a really fun evening. My bed was an air mattress on the floor of the bedroom that was Jon's office and somehow that evening Libna produced an amazing dinner and a lovely breakfast the next morning.

There is something about spending time with young couples in pastoral ministry that is truly refreshing. I was delighted to simply see their passion for reaching people and making a difference in their lives. They were willing to endure less than ideal conditions and awkward challenges to their home life just to be part of the family of God and to serve in a pastoral role.

One of the great challenges that face pastors like Jon is to simply be taken seriously as a leader in churches with long history, well established local leaders, and a past that sees pastors come and go every few years. A relatively inexperienced pastor in their late twenties to mid thirties is going to find it hard to be trusted to lead. ***Often we don't mind engaging a younger physician who comes with the latest technology. We will trustingly get on a commercial plane with a young pilot, but we are reluctant to truly turn the leadership of a church over to any new pastor, especially if they are under 40!*** In my humble opinion we simply have to find ways to work together better. Pastors need to be sensitive to the needs, gifts, traditions, and such in the local church. We need to be willing to work with the team we are given. ***The church, on the other hand, needs to be willing to build trust with new leadership and benefit from new ideas, methods, and the experience that pastor has gained from previous churches or from recent training. The church today is not the same as it was forty, twenty, or even ten years ago. The message should be the same, but the package and the way we deliver it must be very different and always ready for reevaluation.***

Now in my thirty-seventh year of pastoral ministry and thinking back on the changes I have seen seems amazing. I began by typing my own bulletin on a stencil and running it off on an A. B. Dick mimeograph that had to be hand cranked. Some of you will have to Google that just to know what I'm talking about. Google didn't exist back then either, by the way!

Many of the contemporary churches don't even use bulletins any more. They don't communicate with newsletters. Today's churches often communicate through Twitter, Facebook, and My Space. They listen to podcasts and watch clips on YouTube and they text far more than they talk. You can talk about the glory days of MV meetings and six week long evangelistic efforts, and those will still work for some people in some areas, but if we are going to have a church to talk about in another couple of decades we better be willing to embrace, welcome, and get involved with new ideas and ways of reaching young adults.

Jon and Libna were refreshing to share with and there is good reason to have hope in the future leadership of our church with couples like this in our midst. That is not intended in any way to be critical of any of the "older" and "more experienced" pastoral couples I have been with on this trip. That would be shooting myself in the foot for sure wouldn't it? Promise me that you will simply commit to pray for pastors everywhere, and particularly for your own pastor(s).

Well, that finished up week two and after fourteen days on the road I had covered 4,340 miles. The next week would take me to see some great churches, some good friends, and then end with our children in Virginia and West Virginia. See you there.

Chapter the Fourth

The Second Decade

The decade from age 10- 19 was the time when my relationship with my dad turned gradually from fear to rebellion. These years were mixed with happy memories, achievements, and promise, but also with dark thoughts, hatred, and the beginning of a downward spiral into a sense of being completely lost.

One classic story was when I was eleven years old. It seemed my small allowance each week didn't seem to be adequate to meet my sweet tooth. One day I walked the mile or so from our house to the grocery store where we always shopped. Wandering around I found it quite easy to stuff a candy bar in my pocket and walk out the door. About a week later, finding it was so easy, I put two candy bars in and did it without any problem. Through the weeks my brashness increased. Then one day with five or six bars packed away and just heading out the door there was a voice over the loudspeaker, "Bob, check that young man walking out the door." I'm not sure why I didn't run, but instead I just froze. A thousand thoughts raced through my mind and all of them included my dad, so I determined not to reveal my identity. Escorted through the aisles, into the backroom and up the stairs to the manger's office they sat me in a chair.

"What's your name son?"

I made something up.

"Where do you live?"

I told them, "Chicago." Keep in mind that this was in Edmonds, just north of Seattle.

"How did you get out here?"

I said, "I hitchhiked."

These guys were amazing. Somehow they were able to discern that I wasn't being totally honest with them. They went through all the same questions again and I gave them the same answers. After a third time through they said to just sit there and relax because they were going to call a friend of mine.

Wow, that was really surprising because I couldn't figure out how they knew any of my friends. A few minutes later heavy footsteps could be heard coming up the wooden stairs outside of the manager's office and I turned to look right into the gun and the bullets hanging on the waist of the Chief of Police. I knew it was the Chief because he lived just one block from our house, but he didn't recognize me.

He went through similar questions with me and I wasn't any more cooperative than before because I was just so scared of being taken to my father. So, he said that we were going to take a little drive.

I was more than a little self-conscious being escorted through the store by the Chief. We went out the door and into the parking lot where his police car waited. Now desperation was setting in and a plan began to develop. When he opened the door to the back seat I would slide right across, open the other door and run!

Just in case you don't know, it may be helpful information for you to realize that the back seat of police cars have a factory defect. They forgot to install door handles! Now I was stuck. We drove the four or five blocks to the basement of the library where the police station was. Once inside he asked me if there was any change to my story at all and I politely informed him that there was not, at which point he opened a wooden door, behind which was a cell door and he gave me a little nudge into my new room. There was a bunk, a sink, a toilet and a lot of time.

About an hour later I called out through the closed and locked doors, "I'll tell you who I am now."

The answer came booming back, "I don't care now!"

This was not going good!

Sitting there for four hours that dark day. I could hear a variety of conversations between people who came into the station and one-way conversations on the phone. Finally I heard one that caught my attention.

"Edmonds Police Department."

"Yes, could you describe him please?"

"Well, you might want to come on down and take a look at a young man we have in custody."

I was now going to face the judgment. Obviously, as I write this I can do so with a smile on my face and perhaps it will make you smile too, but let me assure you, I was not smiling that day.

Sitting there awaiting my fate I began to process a thought in my eleven-year-old mind. "I will laugh again. It will not be today, and it may not be tomorrow or even the next day, but I will laugh again."

Thinking back on that story I still am amazed at the positive thinking that gave me courage that dark evening. That same exact sequence of thoughts has brought me through several other challenging times in my life. It works.

It wasn't long before my dad's voice could be heard in the outer office. The wooden door was opened and I looked into the eyes of my dad through cell bars. His first words were, "It's a good thing those bars are between us right now." Please bear in mind that a few choice words that were included have been deleted here. The Chief closed the wooden door and said, "Mr. Wray, I think we should spend a few minutes together before your son is released."

A short time later I was indeed released into the custody of my dad. Staying put would have seemed preferable, but I was glad to get whatever was coming over with. We drove home without a word being said and when we got home and into the living room he grabbed hold of me and put me on the floor where he proceeded to kick me several times until my mom made him stop. No broken bones and no horrendous injuries were sustained. I was more scared and humiliated than anything. The very worst part of the punishment was being taken back to the store and having to apologize to the manager. That was also the part that kept me from ever doing it again. Another event that solidified how I would view my dad for the next many years soon followed this event.

Rolly had a very strong work ethic. He never missed work or was late unless he was really sick and I can't recall any time that he was, other than this one experience. My dad was an alcoholic. He had gotten to the point where he came home from work every night and began to drink until he finally passed out on the sofa. My sister and I would do the dishes each night after dinner and we would monitor his drinking and his progress toward oblivion silently through a series of hand signals. When he was finally out we would breathe a sigh of relief and know that we were safe for another night. We would go to bed usually long before he came around and went to bed himself.

One morning my mom told me that dad was sick and wouldn't be able to go to work today and that it would be necessary for me to stay home from school and take care of him. Normally a boy would be only too delighted to get a day off from school, but I did not want to spend the day at home alone with him, however there was no choice. As the day wore on he got worse and worse until he finally told me to call the doctor. When the doctor came and examined him he called for an ambulance to come and take him to the hospital. That was a pretty major event for a young boy. I vividly remember watching the ambulance leave the driveway and watching through the living room window. I got on my knees, watched, and prayed. I prayed that my dad would die.

That is a horrible memory thinking back on it. How could a son have actually done that? I simply knew that my life would be so much easier if my dad was not in it. Rolly had cirrhosis of the liver and indeed his chances of dying were more likely than not, but he did live. He came home a couple of weeks later and the doctor told him that if he ever drank again he would be dead in six months or less, but he picked up right where he left off anyway.

Rolly always drank at home. I only remember him going out to drink this one night and I have no idea what his reasons were. Later there was a knock on the door and the mayor of the town brought my dad up on the front porch and layed him in the living room. To this day I don't know what all happened that led up to this, but I do know that he was completely oblivious to what was going on and that he urinated all over the floor. Then something astonishing happened. My mom, all five foot two of her, came and stood over him and said, "I'm taking the kids and I'm leaving." I absolutely could not believe that she had said this. She had never stood up to him like that before except the night he brought me home from the police station.

My dad stammered out, "No, don't go. Call AA."

A short time later two men came from Alcoholics Anonymous and tried to talk with Rolly, but he wasn't exactly articulate. They told him that if he was serious he should call them again in the morning and they would come back. He did, and they did, and he never took another drink for the last forty-seven years of his life.

As wonderful as this all sounds the immediate effect was not good for the rest of us. My dad went from being a sleepy drunk to being an angry recovering alcoholic and now we had to deal with him every night. It was also very interesting to me that he would drink himself to death and risk losing us all, but the fact that my mom was going to leave him motivated him to make such a drastic turnaround.

By now, at age twelve, one thing was clear in my mind: I didn't want to be anything like my dad and resented any time spent with him. Unfortunately he had me accompany him almost any time he went out. He also had me help him whenever he worked on the car as well as when he did extra auto mechanic work on nights and weekends. I did what he told me to do, cleaning parts and tools, handing tools to him and holding things in position so he could install them. My mind was determined not to pay any attention to the things he tried to teach me and as a result I have basically no mechanical aptitude. I'm sure that is my loss, but that's just the way I purposed to stay outside of the relationship. Was it all my dad's fault? Obviously not, but that's just the way I coped.

My early teen years were relatively uneventful regarding the way things worked at home. School and athletics were my outlets and much focus was poured into the latter. No one can say that I was a scholar, but my grades were good enough and there was also involvement in school politics. In the sports area my opportunity for excellence was definitely in track distance running. I'll talk more about that a little further on.

All the time that my dad was in his alcoholic/atheistic mode my mother was such a saint. She was patient, loving, and Godly. My sister and I went to church with her every Sunday morning and evening and on Wednesday evenings as well. Going to church was great and I loved the people there. It was only there that adult male affirmation was given to me, and the men in that church made a huge difference in my life. ***Most of us men don't realize the opportunity for impact that we have in our relationship with boys and young men in the church or in our neighborhoods.*** I have made a deliberate effort to contact all of those men to let them know what an impact they had on me.

At the age of twelve I responded to my first altar call. The appeal was made on a Sunday night and I went forward and knelt at the altar. A dear man, a Dr. in the church, came and knelt beside me and put his arm around my shoulder. He encouraged me with the words, "Your Heavenly Father is so proud of you right now." His words struck me with incredible impact. I knew that my Father had never and would never accept me and so I was certainly positive that my Heavenly Father could never accept me. As that sweet Dr. prayed for me I knelt there and cursed God for His unwillingness to accept me.

Over the next few years I went forward to literally dozens of altar calls at church, at youth camps and retreats and at campmeetings, but the result was always the same; God simply would never accept me and I grew more and more spiritually disconnected even though the pastor did baptize me, mostly to please my mother. By the age of sixteen I had given up on God although church attendance and youth activities remained a part of my life.

As mentioned previously, athletics were my source of joy and affirmation. I did very well in distance running in both Jr. High and High School. In my sophomore year in High School I set a record in the Seattle school system for the mile by sophomores, running it in four minutes and forty-two seconds. Area coaches were already beginning to talk to me about college scholarship possibilities, but it almost seems that my inner conviction that my dad was right (that I was no good and would never amount to anything) was my destiny. In my junior year there was minimal effort put into track and I only managed to equal the previous year's time, but should have been able to take at least twenty seconds off of it. My senior year I dropped out of track altogether and began smoking and drinking regularly. This was the beginning of my darkest period.

Another change had taken place on the home front. My interaction with Rolly became more and more heated. I was bigger now and bolder in my rebellion. There had been one major incident that doesn't warrant giving the details, but it was a significant event that once again involved the police. Some time after that I ran away from home one afternoon simply leaving a note. Walking sixteen miles from Edmonds to the Seattle bus terminal there was no plan in my mind and not much money in my pocket.

Purchasing a ticket first to Tacoma, just sixteen miles further south, I got off the bus and just walked around the city for a while and then went into a bowling alley and bowled five or six games just to pass some time. Then it was back to the bus station and I purchased a ticket for as far as my money would take me, which was to Portland, Oregon. My arrival in Portland was in the middle of the night and my thought was, "Now what?" The only place I knew to go to in the area was the campus of Warner Pacific College out on SE Division St. and so began the long walk there. It was still dark and raining and it was more than eight miles away. Thinking back about what might have been as a sixteen year old boy walking around large cities on his own I am just so thankful to God for His care even though I wasn't seeing it at that time.

Warner Pacific College is the college that is part of the Church of God denomination and that is the church of my childhood. There were a few of the students there from my home church and one member of the faculty. Upon arrival everyone was still sleeping so I waited outside the locked dormitory until people started moving around. When a young man from my home church saw me he took me to breakfast and then helped me connect with the faculty/administrator that knew me as well. That good man convinced me to allow him to contact my parents and arranged for me to get home just three days after leaving. My parents, especially my dad, couldn't, or wouldn't, understand the feelings and thoughts going through my young and confused mind and, obviously, I couldn't understand or make any sense of them either.

When I returned home our family had a meeting with our family physician and it was decided that it would be best for me to live with my sister and brother-in-law who graciously took me in even though they had a small home and a small child as well. Part way through my Sr. year I did move back home and the separation had been good. Rolly seemed to accept the fact that I was charting my own course now and would soon be going off to college. It seemed to be basically a cease-fire agreement. I would be on my own and he would have me out of his hair.

Looking back on those early and mid-teen years I do remember many good times, even good times with family. But, there were also the memories that my dad never saw me play ball, never saw me run track, never saw me perform in band or choir concerts and simply never took any interest in what I was involved in. Am I bitter? No, there is no bitterness now. You'll have to read the later chapters to see how it all came together, but I was a young man full of mixed emotions and was looking for acceptance anywhere it could be found.

After graduation from Edmonds High School in June of 1964 my next stop was Western Washington State College in Bellingham, Washington. That particular college was chosen for one reason only; my girlfriend was going there. I don't suppose it mattered all that much because getting an education was the furthest thing from my mind. I went there to escape and to be on my own and went through the basic motions of school and picked a major in music education because I had received a scholarship upon graduation from High School that would apply only if I had that major.

My real major emphasis was clearly on parties, fun, and increased access to alcohol even though I was only eighteen. Now starting to smoke heavily and with no thoughts of any athletic endeavors, I think the rest of this decade can simply be summarized as a flurry of wasted time, energy and money with absolutely no real direction or goals. Yes, my academic major was music education, but it was absolutely certain that I was not going to be a music teacher. Here was a young man just going through motions and spinning his wheels. It can only be said that I am a very lucky man to have just survived the activities that filled and endangered my life. The next decade would see me really hit bottom, but also find the Light that would save me from my sins and from myself. What a mighty God we serve!

Chapter the Fifth
The Third Week

Another Monday morning dawned and I was ready to start my third week of the journey. This was really going to be a great segment because of getting to see some dear friends at several stops and ending the week with our son, daughter, daughter-in-law, and three precious grandchildren. So, let's get on the road!

It is about 200 miles from Tuscaloosa, AL to Opelika, which is also in Alabama. It was a pretty straight and brainless shot across I-20, south on I-65 and then north on I-85. Again, I am reminding you that riding the interstate system is not particularly exciting or scenic, but it definitely is the quickest way to reach a destination. I often dreamt of my original desire to ride across the country and never set my tires on an interstate highway. That dream is still there, but will definitely have to wait for some time. Yes, honey, I remember my promise.

Heading south on I-65 brings you into Montgomery where you connect with I-85. As I rode through that great city many thoughts about all of the significant events that had taken place there, particularly with the civil rights movement, flooded my mind. On Feb. 18, 1861 Jefferson Davis was inaugurated as President of the Confederate States right there in that great city.

On March 2, 1955 Claudette Colvin, a teenage black girl refused to give up her seat to a white woman and was arrested. A similar, but more publicized, act took place on Dec. 1 of that same year when Rosa

Parks boarded a bus in Montgomery and refused to give up her seat to a white man. Both of these women and, of course, many others deserve our admiration for their courage. ***We, as Christians, should be filled with that same courage to stand for what we know is right and true.***

It would have been wonderful to have visited some of the historical sites here, but my appointment was waiting and I continued up I-85 to Opelika and Lee Whitman, the pastor there.

OPELIKA, ALABAMA

The Opelika Church is new and is a very nice facility with very nice features for conducting outreach programs. Lee is responsible for three other churches, but two of those are taken care of primarily by Uchee Pines, a fairly conservative self-supporting institution. Even though there is a regional, or black, conference that overlaps the Gulf States Conference, Lee told me that 90% of his membership is black. This tells me that the commonality that we can have in Christ far overrides cultural or ethnic diversity. The simple fact is that the Opelika Church is working.

Lee has been there for over two years, but in the past he has never stayed longer than four years. ***He was recognizing that longer pastoral stays are necessary to build real relationships that lead to growth in the church and in the community. A short stay may be fine if a pastor is focusing on a particular project, such as a new building, but to build trust and true bonding with people a longer period of time is needed.*** I saw in Opelika a church with enormous potential. They are reaching into the community through health and exercise programs. Lee showed me his vision for a hiking and exercise station trail on the church property and I could see tremendous possibilities coming from that.

As I mentioned in an earlier stop, it is not so much what program or what worship style is being used. The key is having people involved in the outreach and in the worship planning that are passionate about what they are doing and whom they are doing it for. Christ reached out in so many different ways. I think this was intended to show us that style and methodology are not the important aspects of mission. His constant was His compassion for the lost wherever He found them and whatever their need.

PEACHTREE CITY, GEORGIA

My next stop was in Peachtree City, GA and was just 70 miles up the interstate. Peachtree City is a suburb of Atlanta and I was really looking forward to connecting with Dave and Debbie Ketelsen. Dave's dad, John, is one of my elders in Napa and John's wife, Sharon, is my treasurer. It is a wonderfully, but amazingly, small world in the Seventh-day Adventist Church family. Dave and Debbie were another pair of very kind hosts for me on this project. It had been another very hot day and I was so glad for a shower immediately upon arrival.

You don't have to sit with Dave for very long to see that he has that passion for people that I referred to just a moment ago. He is a wiry, fit, and super active guy and all of that flows into his ministry. The Peachtree City Church sponsors a 5K run every year that draws about 100 participants. ***Dave and Debbie told me that churches that provide recreational activities as part of their outreach are the fastest growing churches.***

Another very successful event comes in December when they offer their "Truly Christmas" event. The ladies in the church decorate tables and prepare food and their husbands serve a dinner to women in the community. They generally have over 300 women who attend and more than 60% of them are not members.

At Peachtree City every member is encouraged to know the church's mission statement and be involved in a ministry. That mission statement is: "Saved To Love and Serve." Truly that is the intended result of Christ's salvation isn't it? Here the members not only know it, they do it.

Last, but not least, in the area of ideas for connecting, is their annual Visitor's Sabbath. A special program is planned, widely advertised, and carried out. A wonderful fellowship meal is shared and every visitor receives his or her own peach pie. Hey I'd go to church for a peach pie, wouldn't you? Caring about people and reaching out to them exactly where they are and then welcoming them into your fellowship just as they are; these are the tickets to growth.

After another great night's rest and a wonderful breakfast once again I was ready to ride, although a bit worried about riding right through Atlanta's morning rush hour traffic. However, I seemed to be going against the majority of commuters and was also able to ride in the car pool lanes, which is a huge advantage on the bike. Often I had to remind myself that only in California is it legal to ride the white line between the lanes. That doesn't mean it isn't done anywhere else; it just isn't legal.

AUBURN, GEORGIA

It was only 80 miles from Sharpsburg, GA, where Dave and Debbie live, to Auburn, GA to meet with Gary Rustad. I was transitioning from a new facility in a large suburban area to an older church facility that was in a much smaller town and a country setting. The effects of the ministry being done, however, were much the same.

Again, it is fun to see the dynamics of relationships and connectivity within the Adventist Church structure. We first met Gary's dad, Gary Sr., in Hong Kong, where we pastored for six years. We had gone back for a visit and now he was pastoring there. Now Gary Jr. is leading out in Auburn, GA, and doing it very successfully.

Gary has been in Auburn for three years and hopes to stay. This is his second pastorate. As I mentioned, this is an older building set right on the corner of a main intersection and across the street from the fire station. The building is well kept and makes a very nice presentation.

Although there are just under 200 in attendance each week they have to use three other rooms with closed circuit TV. Now that's a nice problem to have! There is strong financial support in the church for scholarships to aid students at their church school as well as for project needs such as carpeting, a roof, and a piano.

Gary has worked hard to build a personal relationship with the mayor and other civic leaders and they have built strong ties with the community at large. During the annual Fall Festival, which occurs right on the street in front of the church, they close church services and set up booths and provide music for the festivities. They work hard to invite community children for Sabbath School. Several cooking and exercise classes are offered throughout the year and the Boy Scouts use the church basement for free.

The biggest challenge in Auburn is to clearly define their future. With a significant ethnic mix with different backgrounds and expectations, he is still working hard to get everyone on board and feeling ownership, but this church is definitely one that is on the move.

Now there were nearly 300 miles to cover to get to my evening destination, which was the Madison Campus Church, just north of Nashville, and the home of Lynn and Lona Schlisner.

I stopped on the way to have lunch with good friends, Steve and Bev Ericson and their daughter Kara. Our friendship dates from way back in the beginning of our ministry in Hawarden, IA. It is wonderful how once you really bond with friends you can go years without seeing each other and yet pick up right where you left off. After nearly 37 years of ministry all across the U.S., and in the Far East as well, we are so rich with friends! It was great to see the Ericsons again and renew that love.

MADISON CAMPUS, TENNESSEE

There were many reasons for looking forward to my time with the Schlisners. First of all, Lynn has done some amazing things during his fourteen years as Lead Pastor at Madison Campus. He has led out in the significant expansion of the church as well as the significant growth in the church family. When he came, there were around 400 attending and 1,100 members on the books. Now there are 800 attending and 1,500 on the books. That means that he has increased the active membership by 400 and they are all staying active.

Lynn is-how shall I say it-unique. When describing him to others I always tell them that Lynn is one of the few people that can make me look fairly normal! Make no mistake, I love this guy. We worked together in the Potomac Conference. We also traveled through Germany, Poland, Czech Republic, Slovakia, and Austria together with our wives, Schlisner's daughter, our daughter, and Len and Karen McMillan. Now that was an adventure, but that is another story.

Lynn is a Viet Nam Vet and a South Dakota farm boy and his members love him and his wife, Lona. He has so many stories to tell, but his greatest story is the gospel of Jesus Christ and he tells that one so well. ***I think it is safe to say that Lynn's greatest asset and strongest***

program for the church is simply his deep and sincere love for the people. The church offers a strong program related to "Celebrate Recovery" and a variety of other programs geared to reach the community. Their outreach is focused not so much on bringing in numbers, but rather on building relationships.

I would ask a special prayer request for Lynn. He has undergone three surgeries for a rare type of brain tumor. Through all of that he has kept up his work for the church, but it is getting increasingly difficult after each surgery. Thank God they are in a place where they have built strong relationships and the church offers tremendous support. ***Results like we have seen at Madison Campus cannot come without long tenure and genuine love. Those are the key ingredients for church growth.*** Programs and innovative outreach are important tools, but long lasting love is the foundation. Next stop, Knoxville, and another set of good friends in the persons of Ed and Cheryl Komorowski.

(As of this writing Lynn has been hospitalized yet again and things have been looking pretty bleak. He is still a fighter and has just been moved to rehab and we are all hopeful that he will be able to maintain some quality life for as long as possible. I have talked with him several times and his outlook is always, always positive, with the full assurance that he is in God's hands, but he has finally had to step back from his position of church leadership.)

KNOXVILLE, TENNESSEE

This was another very easy bike day. It is less than 200 miles from Madison Campus Church to Knoxville and a straight shot on I-40, so I slept in a bit, had a relaxed time with Lynn and still arrived in the mid-afternoon. It was very nice to have the break in the riding intensity and I was looking forward to the next several days.

My first meeting with Ed and Cheryl was when they came from Ohio to the Potomac Conference where I was the Ministerial Director at the time. Before coming to Knoxville two years ago they pastored in Vienna, VA, where I had pastored from '87-'91. ***They did a great job there and contributed significantly to the strengthening of that church through, again, building relationships within the church family and with the community. Jesus did tell us that while we were not to be of the world, we certainly were to be "in" it! Didn't He demonstrate that strongly by the people He constantly connected with?***

In Knoxville Ed is repeating what has worked for him before. It was fun to attend their evening Vacation Bible School program and watch him in action as a participant in the daily skit, playing and teasing with the kids, and interacting with the adult leaders. If you just sit back and watch it doesn't take long to see that Ed and Cheryl are a couple that simply and genuinely love the people God places in their path. They don't focus on number goals. ***I believe that when we focus on goals based in numbers we tend to see people as prospects. God wants us to see them as brothers and sisters and He desires for us to be looking as to how we can best serve them and lead them to a closer walk with Him.***

In Knoxville the church, like so many churches today, is facing financial challenges, but Ed has also demonstrated a good business head in the past and he's not sticking his head in the sand here either. We all need to see our churches stay on good financial footing. We are called to be good stewards not only of the people He has entrusted to us, but also with the gold and silver.

Thursday morning I was off early, but not before Cheryl prepared a bountiful and delicious breakfast to send me on my way. It was a little surprising to find my bike quite wet in the morning so I did a little wipe down and put the thoroughly soaked gel seat pad in the trunk and went on my way. This was going to be a fun day and not a workday!

CHEROHALA SKYWAY/TAIL OF THE DRAGON

It is only about 70 miles from Knoxville, down I-40 and I-75 through Sweetwater, TN and then down Hwy 68 to Tellico Plains, TN. There I met up with David and Vicki O'Guin to fulfill one of my "Bucket List" items. Vicki is an aunt to our daughter-in-law, Jenny, and I performed their wedding just three years ago. They ride a great looking Gold Wing and we were going to spend the day riding the Cherohala Skyway and, best of all, the Tail of the Dragon! We didn't cover such exceptional mileage that day. I think it was less than 300 miles total, but we rode for 14 hours before checking into a motel for the night.

There is no way I can put into words the beauty to be seen on this day's ride. The Cherohala Skyway is loaded with vista points and you just can't possibly stop at them all, but we hit quite a few. It was a beautiful day with just enough overcast to keep the sun from baking you, but no rain. I was really enjoying this and every time I looked at David and Vicki riding along together it made me long for Ingrid to be behind me so that she could drink all of this beauty in. After several hours of leisurely riding and sight seeing we came to Deal's Gap, a motorcycle Mecca if there ever was one.

I had been reading about Deal's Gap and the Tail of the Dragon for years and never thought I would actually have the opportunity to ride it. It must be on every biker's dream list of rides. What makes it so special? Well, try 318 curves in 11 miles! There are two words that come into my mind when I get that picture in my brain. The first is "Wow" and the second is "Caution!"

The first stop was the Deal's Gap Store and facing the challenge of finding a place to park your bike on a sunny day in late June. Thankfully there are enough guys (and gals) taking off to ride the "Tail" that you can move into a spot fairly quickly. What fun to walk through the parking lot and just look at all the varieties of bikes to be seen. Then look at all the variety of humanity that rides them! It was interesting to say the least. We picked up some souvenirs, ate a little lunch, took advantage of some photo opportunities, and we were ready to challenge the Dragon.

I couldn't help but notice a very special tree outside in the parking lot. It is called the "Tree of Shame." On it hangs a wide variety of parts from hundreds of motorcycles that were less than successful in completing the course. I am very happy to report to you that none of my bike parts were injured in the making of this book! We did make an agreement, however, that we would approach this ride sanely and cautiously. We didn't want to be ones holding up traffic, but if a rider or a group wanted to pass we'd just let them go. There were only a couple of bikes that passed. There just aren't many opportunities. I will admit to being just a bit nervous starting out having read many reports and articles and having seen several clips on YouTube about others who were beaten by "The Tail." Just try looking at the variety of crashes available online on You Tube when you type "Tail of the Dragon" into the search area. I quickly found, however, that at a fun, but respectful, pace, this was a delightful run!

We were tempted to go back and do it again, but the surrounding roads are just as much fun and more scenic as well. So, we continued on our way and were quickly reminded that you have to be careful on all the roads. We saw three accidents that afternoon. Two involved bikes and one was a pickup truck. One of the bike accidents looked pretty bad. A car had apparently hit the rider as he left a parking lot or as he was turning into it.

Part of the afternoon was spent riding on the Blue Ridge Parkway, which winds along the crest of the Great Smokey Mountains in North Carolina all the way up to northern Virginia for a total distance of 469 miles of gorgeous scenery. The speed limit is 45 mph so this is not a ride to make good time, but the beauty is worth it! We rode until after it was dark and finally got to a motel in Asheville, NC. We were tired, hungry, and very, very thankful for a gorgeous day and a safe arrival.

The next morning we were on our way fairly early as we had well over 300 miles to cover and we opted to just hop on I-81 and make good time. I was getting excited about our next destination knowing there would be a welcoming committee of three grandchildren. My plans were to stop at the North Valley Church in Roanoke, but it was necessary to get some maintenance work done on the bike and time was running short so I called Pr. Mike Hewitt and made my apologies. Out of the entire trip that was the only appointment that was not kept.

FISHERSVILLE, VIRGINIA/GRANDKIDS

As we rolled into Fishersville, VA we stopped for gas and also made a phone call to our son, Steven, and let him know that I would be there in just a few minutes. We wanted to make sure that the little ones knew that Opa was finally going to arrive. As we came around the last corner and started up the last hill I made sure that they could hear me. What a joy it was to see those two youngest grandkids, ages 4 and 6, jumping up and down as I pulled up. As excited as they were they were still pretty hesitant to run up to that big bike and all the thunderous noise. Once I got off and removed the helmet they were in my arms though and it was so good to be halfway through the ride.

I spent a wonderful weekend with family and friends. We had spent more than five years working in the Potomac Conference office, which is in Staunton, just a few miles away, and so time spent here has a feeling of home to us. I cherished the chance to build Lego cars with our grandson, Beck, and to admire the multiple Princess outfits our younger granddaughter, Inge, modeled and then to just sit and look at our older granddaughter, Emma, who is just growing up way too fast!

I also was glad to have the expertise of extended family that performed a much needed and welcome servicing on the bike. Cory and Dave changed the oil and filter and gave the whole bike a thorough inspection and it was ready to go a good many miles more.

The long weekend break was very welcome and restful although the grandkids do certainly take up a fair amount of energy. We went to a Polo match in Charlottesville on Sunday, which was fascinating, by the way. Then on Monday I went with the kids to swimming lessons and just fully enjoyed family time.

VIENNA, VIRGINIA

On Tuesday I rode up to the Washington, D.C. area to make two more visits to churches and to be there when Ingrid would arrive on Friday. My first stop was Vienna, VA where I had pastored for five years just prior to my time as Ministerial Director for the Potomac Conference. Vienna is just sixteen miles from downtown D.C. and the area, as well as the church, is very beautiful.

An added plus to this visit is that the current pastor is Garry Genser, who came to Vienna from the Fortuna, CA church, and we were already good friends. It is always a strange sensation to walk into a place where you spent many years, but now you are a visitor. The church has been refurbished since we were there and it makes a lovely presentation. ***A hallway surrounds the sanctuary and the classrooms are on the outside perimeter. There are multiple sitting areas as you walk around the building and each has a painting depicting some aspect of Christ's ministry and the whole setting is very inviting.***

I have always loved the sanctuary of the Vienna Church. As you walk in from the back your eyes are drawn upward. Looking above the platform you see the choir loft with three rows rising high. Above that is the baptistery and then high above the baptistery is a large cross. I never tired of looking at the front of that church. The first time I saw it I said, "I can preach here."

I have to share one story from my time in Vienna. I was conducting a baptism one Sabbath morning and the candidate and I entered the water from one side. There are entrances and changing rooms on both sides and my head deacon, Howard Blair, was on the other side. As we entered the water he launched a yellow rubber duck from his side, which proceeded to bob across the water in plain view through the glass panel in front. A chorus of chuckles rose from the congregation and I seriously wished that I could grab Howard and rebaptize him that very day. I might have held him down just a bit longer this time.

One unique outreach being done in Vienna involves the radio station from the campus of Washington Adventist University, WGTS. This station has the second largest Christian radio audience in the U.S. ***Vienna is one of four "Radio Churches" and once or twice a year they host a "Radio Day." On these days they have the radio personalities at the church and, of course, that is advertised and promoted well in advance. This is followed up by a young adult event and that, in turn, is followed by an evangelism event focused on young adults. They have had good response in the recent past and I'm looking forward to seeing how this grows. Good creativity Gary!***

Vienna is also taking advantage of the large number of immigrants in the Washington, D.C. area and offers English as a Second Language classes for the community and this also is having a good response. While this, in itself, is not intended to be evangelistic in nature, it does build

relationships with the individuals and with the community and that is what Christ's method of reaching people is all about.

GENERAL CONFERENCE AND FRIENDS

In the afternoon I rode over to the General Conference Headquarters in Silver Spring, MD. I always enjoy my visits there because of so many friends from our years of ministry working there. I came today particularly to see Don Freesland, who works in the IT Department.

Don was a member of our church when we pastored in Vienna and we shared many great memories together through those years. He was a Snap-On Tools rep when I first met him and was looking for a change. Learning of his computer knowledge I arranged for an interview at the General Conference when it was still in Takoma Park. Well, he knew all the right things and he has been working there ever since and that has been over twenty years. It was so good to see him and have lunch with him and his wife, Shelly. I am even deeply honored by the fact that his son's middle name is Wray.

After this fun interlude I rode back around the Beltway to Falls Church, VA to stay the night with a precious friend, Jeanetta Badgley. She and her husband, Roy Harding, were members in Vienna also and have remained close friends through the years. It was a sad day when Roy passed away while we were pastoring there. He was a sweet, sweet man. A few years later Jeanetta met Bill Badgley and she found real happiness again.

I'll never forget that wedding. I performed it and we hosted it in our home in Staunton, VA when I was working in the Conference Office there. They stood in our living room with Jeanetta's daughter, Heidi, as witness and I got to the vows. I somewhat teasingly asked her if she promised to love, honor and obey and without a moment's hesitation she said, "Absolutely not!" It took us a few minutes to get our momentum going again after that, but they have been happily married ever since.

Everything, both bad and good, is temporary in this life. I went with Jeanetta to visit Bill in a nursing home as he suffers from Alzheimer's. He did seem to remember me and he certainly knew Jeanetta although she tells me that sometimes he doesn't. A few months later we got a phone call telling us that Bill had passed away. Won't it be grand when Jesus comes and these scenes of life will be no more?

NEW HOPE CHURCH, FULTON, MARYLAND

Wednesday found me riding around the Beltway one more time and heading toward Fulton, MD to meet with David Newman at the New Hope Church. David has a rich background in ministry and I have always had a great respect for him. He was the editor for Ministry Magazine for several years and returned to pastoral ministry after that. He has been with the New Hope Church for more than seven years now and this was truly one of my most exciting and inspiring visits.

Over the past seven years they have doubled their membership and attendance. In fact their membership and attendance are the same, which is about 700! When someone is baptized, or transfers in, he or she must attend a 3-hour "Entrance To New Hope" seminar that is provided every other month. In this program they are introduced to the philosophy of the church explaining that their focus is on the gospel and not on the lifestyle growth of the members. They clearly explain that they are Christians first and Seventh-day Adventists second. Their target on Sabbath mornings is the unchurched and 12% of their attendance is made up of these. More than half of attendees are not members of New Hope. The median age of the church is 26, whereas the median age for Adventists in North America is 55. New members are also linked to a mentor.

Obviously something is out of the norm here. What makes the difference? It is not the fancy facilities. While the church makes a nice, well-kept appearance it is simply a steel building with ample office and meeting space. ***The sanctuary is not fancy. It is comprised of a large concrete floored worship area with a large, versatile platform and a portable baptistery in the middle of the room. The chairs are moveable to accommodate a wide variety of worship opportunities. It is clear that their emphasis is on people rather than on aesthetics. I loved the "Ask Me" desk in the entryway. A simple, but well marked, information booth is staffed throughout the morning including during the worship services.***

Some of the things that seemed to stand out in the brief time I had to visit with David and his office staff are that things here are not set in concrete. One word that would describe New Hope is "innovative." ***They are constantly not only willing to change, but eager to do so. They thrive on creativity. Another feeling I quickly got was a huge and sincere sense of welcome, acceptance, and caring. I experienced this even on a weekday from the office staff. The two Administrative Assistants, Prithy David***

and Lynn Ekelof, made me feel very welcome and they didn't know who I was, or why I was there. If I got that kind of treatment during working hours just think of what a Sabbath morning must be like! I do believe that when people come to check out a new church, that is what they are looking for most. The old saying, "They don't care how much you know until they know how much you care" is absolutely still true.

I assure you that the New Hope Church has not "watered down" or "whitewashed" the core beliefs of the Seventh-day Adventist Church. They have simply put first things first and it is working and is one of the few fast, but steadily, growing SDA churches in North America. This is definitely one church to check up on from time to time.

MORE FAMILY AND FRIENDS

Now I had a chance to meet Ingrid's cousin, Bruno Heidik, and his wife, Tuulikki, for lunch and a brief chance to just catch up. I love visiting with them and Bruno and I can share stories of ministry as he served in the United Methodist denomination for many years and still stays active with writing and counseling. In his early years of ministry he pastored in the Seventh-day Adventist work. When we first met he was just transitioning out of our denomination and I was just beginning and was a new convert as well. Some of those early conversations were a bit tense and uncomfortable for me as I felt the need to defend my new faith. Through the years we have grown closer and closer and we share the fundamental similarities we have in our love for Jesus and we have dropped all defensiveness. I feel that we have both grown through the years and have developed a deep and sincere respect for each other.

The rest of this middle week was spent with family. I went, Wednesday afternoon, to meet with our daughter, Julie, at her work. She was so happy to show off her Papa and his motorcycle. That evening I stayed with Norm and Carol Wootton, Julie's in-laws, and we always have so much fun.

We marvel at how Julie and her husband, Will (known to us as T), got together. Wootons were all members of the Vienna Church when we pastored there and Will saw Julie that first Sabbath and was smitten.

It seems like he was constantly finding an excuse to be at our house. Usually it was under the guise of riding bikes with our son, Steve.

Now I just have to stop and share another personal story. One evening he decided to come and visit Julie, but he didn't want to let the whole house know. He knew which bedroom was hers and he began to toss pebbles against the upstairs window. What he didn't know was that Julie and her grandmother, Hanna, had just traded bedrooms. He also didn't realize that everyone was gone that evening except Hanna. She was more than a little frightened by all of this and, of course, had no idea who was throwing rocks at her window. She threw open the window and called out, "Who's is there? Steven, get the gun!" She couldn't identify the backsides of the young man running for his life down the driveway. When I performed their wedding three years ago my opening line as Julie and Will came to stand before me was, "You again! Steven, get the gun!"

Thursday was also spent with Julie and we rode the bike through the beautiful countryside of West Virginia, Virginia, and Maryland. Julie is my frequent biking partner and has ridden many extended trips with me. She got her first love for riding with me when we pastored in Coos Bay, OR and we would ride the dirt bikes over the sand dunes with her sitting in front of me on the gas tank and holding on to the cross bar section of the handlebars. We would climb hills and speed through rough trails and at the end she would always say, "Do it again Daddy, faster!"

INGRID!!!

Finally, Friday morning dawned and I was at the airport to welcome my sweet wife, Ingrid, for a brief break in the action and a long weekend with kids, grandkids, and family. I can't begin to tell you how good it was to see her and put my arms around her again. She has been such a good sport and supporter of all my "ideas" through more than thirty-six years of ministry. She had bunionectomy surgery just three weeks before and had three screws put into her foot. She was in a walking boot and I know she was still hurting, but she had come anyway and I was happy!

We spent the weekend back down in Fishersville, VA with Steve, Jenny, and the grandkids and it was wonderful. What fun we had! That visit was short, but sweet, and on Sunday we went back up to Inwood, WV to stay with Norm and Carol Wootton. Monday morning I was up very early as I had a long day's ride ahead of me to begin the trip back home. Ingrid flew out that evening and spent the day with Julie shopping. She had to do something to get even with me!

I now had put 6,200 miles on the bike since I left home. I knew the routine by now and was looking forward to many of the visits already scheduled on the return route. There would be stops at several churches where I had pastored previously as well as some key places in SDA history. I was glad that all had been safe thus far and was already looking forward to returning home. The weather had been mostly good and it is a blessing I didn't know what was in store for me. Thanks for riding with me this far.

Chapter the Sixth

The Third Decade

At last, I was twenty-one and could drink legally. The only difference now was that I could go into any establishment and not worry about being asked for ID or being caught in a surprise visit by the liquor control agents. By this time I was drinking heavily and it was having an effect on all aspects of my life.

The other thing that happened when I turned twenty-one was that I could get married without my parent's consent. My dad had sworn that he would never allow me to marry prior to that age. So, shortly after that birthday I was married to my high school girlfriend. Probably we got married simply because everyone expected us to. We really did enjoy being together, but we had not put any serious thought into our future although she was much more structured and self-disciplined than I was.

The summer before the wedding I decided to drop out of college. I knew I didn't want to teach music and had no other direction in mind. My first full time job was as a Fuller Brush Salesman. Some of you will recall those good old days when the Fuller Brush representative would show up at your door with a free sample of some household product and a carrying case full of products to show.

I actually did pretty well at that, but after a few months grew tired of it. Perhaps the end of summer and the rains returning to the daily routine in the Seattle area had something to do with it. Looking back on it all, the reality was that this was the beginning of a pattern where

I would work at a job for about six months and then either grow tired of it or lose it due to my problems with alcohol.

The next job was with Sherman & Clay Music in Bellevue, Washington, a suburb of Seattle. My background in music opened that door and I became the manager of the musical instrument department and focused on selling guitars and amplifiers, but also got to sell a few pianos and organs. This was actually a very good position with a good future, if only I had stayed with the program.

It was while I was working in Bellevue that I got married. My wife was finishing up her senior year at Western Washington State College in Bellingham and we rented a house in Marysville, which gave each of us about an hour commute each morning and evening. We did that for a few months and then I transferred to the Sherman and Clay store in Bellingham and that made things a lot easier. It also put me back in the environment of my old friends and I resumed my heavy drinking habits.

Next on the job list was an opportunity to become a management trainee with J C Penney's right there in Bellingham. This truly was a great opening with wonderful possibilities. I got along well with everyone there and was making good progress, but my drinking was getting out of control and was affecting my work and after about six months I was let go. That was the first time in my life that I had been let go and was without employment. I went back and talked to the manager at Sherman & Clay and he knew the owners of a welding supply firm in town and knew that they needed to hire someone. The phone call and the introductions were made and a day after being let go I was a truck driver carrying compressed gases.

My main job now was to come into work as early as I wanted to and load the truck with the empty oxygen, acetylene, argon, nitrous oxide, and other miscellaneous tanks. Some of these stood about five feet tall and I got to the point where I could roll two at a time up and down ramps and into various warehouses. I eventually even got fairly good at doing three at a time, but the owners frowned on the high risk of dropping one off of the truck.

After loading the truck I drove the empty tanks from Bellingham to Seattle and exchanged them for full ones and drove back. Whenever I was back and unloaded I was done for the day. Usually this got me off of work by three in the afternoon. At that point I headed for my favorite tavern where I stayed most of the evening and often until closing time at 2 am. This, obviously, was not doing me any good and it certainly wasn't helping our young marriage.

To make my situation even worse my routine became to eat breakfast on the way down to Seattle. Breakfast consisted of a dozen powdered donuts and a quart of half and half. I don't believe that qualifies as health food. Lunch on the way home was worse as I would drink a full six-pack of beer. This was not one of my brighter habits as beer and a truck loaded with full flammable and explosive gases do not make a very healthy environment. I can only thank God that He allowed me to even survive these years bent on self-destruction.

After several months I got antsy again and left the truck driving position to sell life insurance for Fidelity Union Life. They had a special policy that was targeted to college seniors and I focused on the campus at Western. The problem with this, and every other job or relationship that I had was that I never made the commitment to take life seriously. I was floundering big time and was beginning to have some pretty serious depression issues. I definitely did not like the person I had become.

A few months later my wife graduated and got a teaching position in the area just south of Seattle. I transferred with Fidelity Union Life to the University of Washington Campus and was doing quite well. Things at home were not all that well, however, and things in my mind and my attitude were not good at all. A few months later I left the life insurance business behind and moved on again. This time it was to a trade I had used as a part time job in college before. I was hired as a crew chief for a company that did inventory for grocery stores, drug stores, lumberyards, and a variety of other retail businesses.

This was actually a very interesting job and provided a lot of variety. The schedule was intense at certain times in a quarter and very relaxed in others. We traveled throughout Washington and Oregon and to this day when I walk into a grocery store I look at the shelves to see how easily the items could be counted. Because of the variety, the travel, and the opportunity to absolutely lose myself in the job for weeks at a time, this was a good job for me, but I continued to drink and smoke heavily and spent little time at home no matter what the schedule was.

We had married in the fall of 1967 and in late 1970 I simply got up one night and announced that I was leaving. I grabbed a few things and just took off. I don't even remember where I went that night. I know I slept in the car somewhere until I went to work the next morning. After that I stayed with a good friend I had shared housing with back in Bellingham who now lived near the University of Washington. So much of this time is a blur. I wasn't making sense or thinking rationally and I was deep into self-loathing.

My real problem was that I had become my father. I hated my father. I hated his drinking and his heavy smoking. I hated his lack of caring about those he should have loved and I hated his attitude. Now, everything that I hated about him I had incorporated into my own life and more, and now I hated myself as well. I can't think of a darker time in my life.

As I look back on all of this from the perspective of forty years later I marvel that I got through it. I still feel pain in my heart for all the hurt I caused so needlessly. I know this was hard for my family and it was certainly hard for my wife and her family. I know it takes two to make things work, but I am not being unrealistic to place the overwhelming majority of the blame on my own shoulders for my choices and my lack of maturity.

My supervisor couldn't help but notice the changes taking place within me and offered me the opportunity to transfer to the Portland, Oregon office in order to have a change in surroundings. I jumped at the chance and moved immediately while the divorce I had filed for worked through the necessary steps.

I am moving rather quickly through all of this because I don't want this part of my life to be focused on in any way. I am not proud of these years, but I do want to show the low point of life I had descended to when God began to find a way to reach down and lift me up. Now we get to the fun part of the story and the miracle of how God can find us anywhere and lead us from there to a marvelous homecoming.

My first weekend in Portland I was lonely, having only briefly met some of my new work associates and I had no friends in town. On Friday night I determined that I would go out, but had no idea of where to go. I didn't want to simply go to a tavern and drink by myself so I looked through the newspaper to see if there might be anything of interest. Glancing through the entertainment section I found an announcement about a dance for singles that would take place at a hotel near the Portland Airport and so I thought that might be a place to start. I managed to find the location, parked my VW bug, and ventured in to have a look around.

As I peeked in through the doors, debating to see if I really wanted to part with the three dollar entrance fee, I didn't spot any particular persons of interest, obviously checking to see if I saw any nice looking young ladies. I didn't.

I went back out to my car thinking of finding a bar by myself, but I really didn't want to do that. So, I thought I'd go ahead and go back in and perhaps I could at least make a few friends. Maybe I would find some guys who liked to fish and could share some good information on rivers in the area.

I went back inside, paid my entrance fee, walked into the ballroom and immediately saw a young lady on the other side of the room that looked like a definite person of interest and made me forget about fishing altogether. She was sitting at a table with several other young men, but there was another seat available and I took it. After a few introductions I asked her if she would like to dance and she graciously said that she would. Of course, what she couldn't have known was what a horrible dancer I was!

Through the evening we danced a few times and would return to the table to talk with the others. During one of the dances I ventured to ask her how old she was. (I never said I was bright!) She, in turn asked me how old I was. I told her I was 24 and again asked how old she was. Her reply was, "Too old for you!" Now, I want you to know that was a gross exaggeration as she is only slightly older than I am and looks much younger! In fact, on subsequent dates if we went to a location where alcohol was served she would always be asked for ID and I never was.

It really wouldn't have mattered anyway because I could never talk her into having a drink.

The evening wore on and I became aware that she had already agreed to go get something to eat with another friend there and so I had better do something if I wanted to see her again, which I definitely did. Taking out my business card and handing it to her with the clever announcement that, "This is ladies choice week and you can call me and ask me out anytime this week," I mentally patted myself on the back at being so clever. She took my card and thanked me. Then she turned it over and wrote her phone number on the back. I was thinking I had it made until she then took the card and handed it to the guy sitting on the other side of her. Then it was time to go and she smiled at me, got up, and left with another guy. Now she didn't have my information and I didn't have hers. She will tell you now that this other guy was just an acquaintance that needed to talk and had no romantic interest. Well, you couldn't have sold that story to me that night.

I wasn't about to give up quite that easily. I did remember her name and took a chance to see if she might be in the phone book. As luck (or God) would have it I did find her name even though she had recently moved to a different Portland suburb. I called her on Sunday and made her an offer she couldn't refuse, telling her I was bowling in a league on Tuesday night and asking her if she would like to come and watch. Wouldn't you say that was a pretty exciting offer? Well, she said that she would, and she did.

She also filled me in on some other details going on in her life at the moment. She also was going through a divorce and she had two boys, ages three and five. She probably thought that would be the end of our connection, but I don't think there was a moment's hesitation, assuring her that I still wanted to see her again.

I need to help you understand some things at this point. You can probably guess by now that this woman was going to become my wife, and I am thrilled to tell you that you are right and that we celebrated our 39th anniversary last May 15.

I can also tell you that neither one of us had any intention of getting involved in any kind of a serious relationship. This young lady, Ingrid, had gone to that dance on a Friday night at the insistent urging of a colleague at work who had to welcome and register guests and didn't want to go alone. Ingrid explained that she was not interested in going to a dance and that it was Friday night. Ingrid had grown up as a Seventh-day Adventist in East Germany. Some things had happened that had shaken her faith somewhat. Her husband had just left her with two children and her father had recently been killed in an auto accident. She was searching for understanding and admits that she was somewhat careless in her decisions for a short time. I tell her that God is making her pay for the rest of her life by being married to me.

Back to the story, I went to pick her up on Tuesday evening, rang the doorbell and was greeted at the door by a great looking five year old boy who took one look at me and gave me a straight on punch in the belly. What he was trying to tell me was that his father had left them and if I had any intentions of spending time with his mom I was going to have to deal with him. That little five-year-old is now forty-six; over six foot five and weighs over 250 pounds. If I hurt his mom I still have to answer to him. If he's not available, his "little" brother is also about six foot five and is ready to back up the threat.

In spite of the very informal setting we did have a good time that evening and I asked if she and the boys would like to go to the ocean on Sunday. She was delighted that I wanted to include the boys. So, on Sunday morning I arrived to a nice pancake breakfast and off we went toward the beach. I stopped at a convenience store on the way and bought a bag of my favorite snack for all of us to enjoy. That was a nice large bag of pork rinds. Upon returning to the car there was a health lecture from the back seat on the evils of pork. This was all new to me, but I listened as I ate the whole bag myself.

We all did have another wonderful time together and Ingrid asked me if I would like to go to church with them next weekend. I had grown up going to church regularly, as I have shared previously, and so, quickly said that I would be delighted to pick them up next Sunday morning and asked what time would be best. The answer, of course, was that I would need to pick them up on Saturday morning and, honestly, my first thought was, "They must live a really long way from the church!"

This was my first exposure to a Seventh-day Adventist Church. In fact I had never heard of them before. My first worship experience was not at all positive. First of all I felt quite conspicuous walking to church on Saturday morning. Then there was the problem with the message. The pastor felt called to give his congregation a reminder about Sabbath observance. All I got from the message was that I shouldn't be eating in a restaurant after church on Sabbath and that I shouldn't be playing golf in the afternoon. My thought was, "If I am willing to come to your church and even put a dollar in the offering plate, what right do you have to tell me where I can eat and what I should do with the rest of my day?" As I look back on the experience after nearly forty years in Adventist ministry I'm not so sure that those weren't valid questions. I don't think it is my job on Sabbath morning when our doors are open to so many visitors to tell you what to eat or how to spend Sabbath afternoon. I think that is something you should discuss with God and learn in private studies.

Well, I remember telling Ingrid that I would never be setting foot in another Seventh-day Adventist Church. I'm sure she felt bad about that, but she didn't say anything and we continued to date. About a month later she got me to agree to try another church in Beaverton and I did go. This was a much more positive experience and I attended with her once in awhile after that.

The next few months were busy with work, getting to know each other better, and working through the final steps of both divorces. I know this sounds like a very shaky beginning and as I look back on it I marvel at how it came together. Within just a few months we were talking about getting married and I must say that Ingrid's mom and sisters were not exactly excited about the prospects. In fact, the pastor that we eventually contacted to perform the wedding had some serious doubts.

Interestingly, a woman who worked with Ingrid had a brother who was a minister for the Church of God. It turned out that he was also a youth pastor in my home church when I was growing up. He met with us and had us take the Taylor-Johnson Temperament Analysis test and then he expressed his reservations. The fact that we were both just recently divorced and that there were children involved, added to the reality that we were coming from two different religious backgrounds and two different cultural backgrounds added up to his opinion that we really should stop and think twice or maybe even three times about this. He did agree to do the service if we decided to go forward, but he made it clear that he did not think it was a good idea. Well, thirty-nine years later we are still married and I've been in ministry for thirty-seven of those years. I'm beginning to think he may have been wrong although, based on the facts, he said the right things.

Ingrid's family, as I mentioned, were equally concerned. Her mom and one sister did come up for the wedding, but I know they had some heart to heart talks with her and justifiably so. There were the religious and cultural issues, with her family having immigrated from Germany along with the recent divorces and the children. Also I was smoking and drinking on top of it. This was not exactly what this strong Seventh-day Adventist family was hoping for. Never the less, the wedding did happen on May 15, 1971 in a little church in Aloha, Oregon. We took a two-night honeymoon to Vancouver, B.C. and the boys were not too happy that they couldn't go along.

One of the good things that happened right away was that I cut way back on my drinking. I now had someplace that I really needed and wanted to be when I wasn't at work. So many things were different now. It seemed as if I had stepped into another world and I realized that many things from my past, including friends, were not necessarily things that I needed to hang on to. There were so many changes that I had never anticipated. Ingrid was always very patient with me. She didn't preach about alcohol or about the smoking. She did draw the line at smoking in the apartment. Often times my work involved all night inventory sessions for large stores and I would come home early in the morning having smoked a couple packs of cigarettes that evening. As I came in the house I would just hear this gentle voice say, "Please just leave your clothes in the laundry room."

Ingrid also led me gently into many other new experiences. She always made sure we had prayer at our meals and that the boys had worship every evening with some Bible stories. The Bible stories were not all new to me, but the purposefulness of making them a part of daily life was.

Within a month or so I came upon a truly great opportunity. Bank of America was hiring management trainees. I had enough experience in the business sector that they were willing to put me into their program. I guess they didn't check all my past references too closely. They told me that I would be placed either in Eureka, California or Ukiah, California. We hoped it would be Ukiah because Ingrid's oldest sister and her family were there. Thankfully that was how it turned out and we moved down there in June. Looking back it is so easy to see God's hand in this whole process.

The management training position was very good and I was headed toward a very solid career in banking. We also got regularly involved in the Ukiah Seventh-day Adventist Church now and, I must say, that church family was marvelous. They took me in and loved me just the way I was. They soon learned that I had a background in music and invited me to sing in their choir. I came to choir practice every week and nobody ever said a word about the pack of cigarettes in my pocket. They even got us involved with the Pathfinder Club. Two events related to that stand out in my mind.

The Pathfinders had a campout one weekend and we were going along to help. One of the leaders asked me if I would teach the Sabbath School Lesson to the Pathfinders and I said that I would. He told me that the lesson was about Ellen Harmon. I just looked at him and asked, "Who is that?" "Oh," he said, "that was Ellen White's maiden name." I was still confused as I replied, "And who is Ellen White?" He just handed me the lesson book and told me to read it before the weekend.

A little later that summer the Pathfinders were in a parade for the 4th of July. They had three flatbed trailer floats depicting the activities of working together, playing together, and worshiping together. I was placed on the float representing worshiping together and was role cast as the preacher behind the pulpit. It seems that somebody had a vision!

In our little apartment there in Ukiah Ingrid made sure that we had worship every evening and I would read to the boys from "The Bible Story" set that I am sure is familiar to every Adventist family. One night I read something about the creation of the world that didn't set right with me and I got quite upset. I remember tossing the book aside and saying that I wasn't going to read any more of this nonsense. Then I told Ingrid that this was all getting a bit too much and that I would love to have a chance to let the pastor know just what I thought about some of these things. I said that I could sure set him straight on several issues. With that I left to attend a bank training class that was held two nights a week.

During the break in the class that evening I went out to smoke, as usual. As I lit that cigarette and drew in the first smoke a pain shot through my chest. I had never experienced that before. A couple more inhales produced the same result and finally I just put it out. On the way home after class I lit up another one and had the same results. There was no pain breathing when I didn't smoke, but every breath of tobacco smoke caused pain. Arriving at home that evening I wasn't in the best of moods. That was when Ingrid shared with me the good news that the pastor was willing to come over the next night. I asked her why he was coming and she simply reminded me of my desire to set him straight. I thought, "OK, and I'll be ready for him too."

The next evening Pastor J. Wylan Wood did show up. We chatted for a few minutes and then I let him have it, going on and on about the age of the earth and dinosaurs, and Sunday, and a host of other subjects on which surely I knew more than him. I must have talked for fifteen or twenty minutes during which he just sat with such a pleasant expression on his face. When I stopped to inhale he just smiled and said, "Marvin, you have raised some excellent questions and there certainly is not time tonight to do justice to them, but I have a member who would be anxious to come and go through each one of those questions and listen to what you have to say." Well, I was just suckered into my first set of Bible studies just as quick as a wink.

Dick Metzler came over just a few nights later and we began to study. He was so patient and kind and sensitive without being at all condescending. He just took me where I was and gently led me step by step. Both of these gentlemen have passed away now, but their work is still going on. I also want to tell you that I continued to try to smoke over the next few days and every time I got exactly the same feeling.

After a few days of this I just gave up and never smoked again. I don't know what Ingrid was praying, but something was working.

The studies continued for several weeks and then we were invited to a musical program at the Ukiah Church. A new singing group had formed out of Oregon and they were presenting a concert. That night I met Max Mace and the Heritage Singers for the first time. It was a night that changed my life completely.

I did love music and the Heritage Singers knew how to present it. Oh, they were considered by many to be too modern and worldly, but they were speaking to my heart. I absolutely loved every song and wished that the concert would never end. Of course, it had to end eventually, but before it did Bill Truby sang "The King Is Coming" and then he gave an appeal. I didn't call this an appeal then. I knew it as a good old-fashioned altar call and that was the last thing in the world that I wanted to sit through. My mind immediately went back to those altar calls when I was a boy. I remembered how I hated them because I always wanted to go forward and every time I did I knew that my Heavenly Father could never accept me because I knew my earthly father never could.

I sat through that appeal knowing that it was never going to end. Ingrid recalls that I nearly crushed her hand as I nervously wrestled with God. I prayed silently, "Lord, I can accept you right here. I don't need to go forward." I don't know where I remembered it from, but the words came back, "If you can't stand for me here, I can't stand for you there."

After what seemed like eternity I got up and walked the long walk down to the front of the church. No one else had come forward. As I walked down there I had a little conversation with God. It went like this: "If you don't let me know that you accept me right now I will never do this again." I'm not sure that's a nice way to talk with God, but I want to tell you that I was flooded with a sense of warmth that I can still recall to this day. I knew that I had been accepted and I was a changed man. I never smoked again and I never drank again. I remembered my dad's experience and some of the things I heard then and I talked to some people at the bank who were in AA and got some good help from them.

I was so excited about this new experience and I wanted to keep on experiencing it. We learned the schedule of the Heritage Singers and went to several other concerts in the northern California area. I talked to them after one of those concerts and they told me that they were going to be singing at the Pacific Union College Church soon and asked if I would be willing to share a short testimony. Thinking that the Adventist church system was rather small and that Pacific Union College would be a small school I thought I could do that. What a surprise I had when I entered the huge sanctuary of that church and saw that it was packed full and we had to stand on a side aisle. I was filled with two clear thoughts. First, I was really scared. Second, I knew that I was supposed to be at this school. You see, as a boy growing up in the Church of God, unacceptable to God, I had a deep desire in my heart to be a minister. Now I knew exactly what God wanted me to do.

On the way back home to Ukiah from Angwin, California I drove quietly. After some time I spoke to Ingrid, who was in the back seat of our VW bug with the two boys. Her mother was in the front. I asked her, "What would you think about being a pastor's wife?" There was no verbal response, but when I looked back I could see the tears in her eyes and her mom had them too. I had my answer and I knew a whole new life was opening up before me.

We shared the news with family and with some of the church members. Of course they were pleased, but I think many of them must have wondered if this was something that would last. This was happening awfully fast. I have to tell you that I wondered if it would last. I certainly knew my track record of not keeping jobs for more than six months. We had only been married for six months! But, I knew that this was God's calling and we moved forward.

Dick Barron, a well known evangelist, was a good friend of the family. He had done the funeral for Ingrid's father just a couple of years before. When he heard about my experience he came by to encourage me and offered to fly me from Ukiah to Angwin and help me make some contacts there. As it turned out he wasn't able to do that, but the fact that he wanted to help me was a great boost to my courage.

The events of the Heritage Singer's concert, the trip to PUC, and the clear sense of calling to ministry all came about in November of

1971. Ingrid and I went down to Angwin, to check things out and try to make some connections. What happened over the next few weeks is simply a marvelous series of miracles and I hope you don't mind me taking the time to share these events.

Our main concerns at this point were to find housing, a job for Ingrid and a part-time job for me, and to get registered for school. Of course one big underlying concern was money, since we didn't have anything at all in savings.

I went first to the College Market and met with the manager, Lester Birney. I shared with him a little of my story and also my background in inventory experience. He very graciously offered me the opportunity to work as many hours as I could manage starting as soon as I was settled. It is a fun side note to tell you that his son, Andy and his family are now members of our church in Napa.

Ingrid applied with the Bank of America office on campus and they were very interested in hiring her. They explained that her initial training would be done just down the hill at the St. Helena branch and that her hours would be Monday through Friday until closing. This, obviously, was going to present a test as during the winter months that would cross over into the Sabbath hours. She didn't say anything immediately, but we had no question as to what our decision would be and so we prayed that God would take control of the situation and we promised Him that we would be faithful. Just a day or two later we got a call that the invitation to work at the bank was official, but that the training had been switched to the Angwin branch and that work would end on Friday afternoons as the bank was closed. So, God began to strengthen my faith one step at a time. He was far from finished.

Our next step was to find housing and we met with the PUC Director of Housing, Joe Gorbea, and he certainly was helpful and tried to be encouraging, but he simply told us that there was absolutely no housing available on campus or in the area. He said that perhaps something would open up in the break between quarters and that he would let us know if anything became available. I told him that I appreciated his help, but that we would continue to look and find our own housing. He wished us luck.

We walked down the hill to the College Market to take a look at the bulletin board to see if anything was advertised there for housing, although Joe had assured us that there was nothing there because he checked it daily. As we walked in we saw someone putting a card up on the board. When they left we went and looked and found a 3 X 5 card advertising a house for rent for $250 a month. That may sound reasonable now, but that was more than we could pay at that time. Let me tell you how our rent budget got established.

As we prepared to move from Ukiah, with no money for college, we decided we could sell a few things. Keep in mind that we really didn't have all that much to sell. We thought we could live without a freezer. That was a decision we later came to regret, but it was all God's timing. We called a used appliance store that advertised that they would buy appliances. The owner came out and looked at our freezer, which was a very good one. In fact, he said, it was better than anything he carried and would not work with his inventory. We told him a bit of our journey and why we were moving and he wished us well. Two days later I got a call from a man who said he was interested in our freezer. I hadn't placed an ad yet and I asked him how he knew we had a freezer for sale. He said that the used appliance store he went to had several nice freezers for sale, but that the owner told him that the freezer he wanted was at our house and gave him our address. He immediately paid us $175 and took the freezer off our hands. We now knew that we could rent a house for that amount. The problem was that the ad on the card (which we removed from the bulletin board) said the rent was $250. No problem for God, right?

I stood on the porch of the White Cottage Ranch talking to Mrs. Watson about her house. Again, I told her about our experience and that I was coming here to prepare for ministry. She said that the big house across the drive had been empty for six months and they had not been able to rent it. I don't know where they had advertised it, but nobody knew about it. Without my saying anything at all about our budget she continued to talk and said that she and her husband had just decided that since it had been empty for so long they would rent it for $175 a month. Well, my faith was growing by the day. Now there was just the little problem of tuition.

In order to enroll for the Winter quarter I needed to come up with $500. That's not such a dramatic amount except for the problem that we didn't have it. By early December Ingrid had already gone down to Angwin to begin work at the bank and she stayed with friends that we had there. I was finishing up details back in Ukiah. I had given my three-week's notice at the bank there and they told me that as a management trainee I wasn't vacating a spot that would leave them short handed and so they just sent me on my way with their blessing. I was anxious to get down to PUC and get settled, but we needed to come up with that money somehow.

Ingrid and I talked on the phone one evening and decided that we really didn't need to have the Magnavox color TV and stereo console. We wouldn't have time to watch it anyway, but it was a lovely piece. We prayed together over the phone that God would help us to sell it and to have the money needed to enroll. Within just a few minutes of that conversation and prayer the phone rang and it was one of the church members from Ukiah, Dwayne Witzel. He said that he had heard we were moving to PUC and he was wondering if we were selling any of our household items. I told him that we were only selling one more piece and what it was. He was excited and said that was exactly what they were looking for and asked if he could come over that night and see it. He was there in less than a half hour and paid in cash. You wouldn't like to know how much he paid would you? That's right, it was $500 and we moved the next weekend.

Everything had fallen into place, and you have to know that God's hand was in all of that. Ingrid had work. I had work, and we had a place to live. This wasn't just a place to live, mind you, we had a three bedroom, two bath house on two thousand acres! Can we say, "God is good?" Now all I had to do was start school.

I'll never forget that first day of classes. I was excited and scared all at once. My very first class was Daniel and Revelation, taught by Dr. Leslie Hardinge. Keep in mind that this was now the second quarter of the year and I was listed as a Senior Theology Major in this class with other Junior and Senior Theology Majors. The big problem was that I had to look up the books of Daniel and Revelation in the table of contents because I had no idea as to where they were in the Bible.

That first class I remember Dr. Hardinge was talking about the Battle of Armageddon. By the time class was over I was pretty sure that it had already started. I remember walking out of class and grabbing the arm of Ted Allen, who had known Ingrid for several years and was a Theology student as well, and I asked him if we believed that Battle of Armageddon stuff. He assured me that we did and I thanked him reluctantly. I knew right then that I had made a huge mistake in heading down this road.

That afternoon I went up to Irwin Hall and found the office of Dr. Hardinge. He welcomed me in and I began to explain my mistake. I told him that I was in way over my head and would never be able to finish his class. He patiently asked me some questions, as he didn't know me at all, and I told him about my recent conversion and my sense of call to ministry. He just smiled and told me this; "I will do something for you that I cannot do for every student, but if you will simply attend class and do the assigned work to the best of your ability I will promise that the door to my office and the door to my home will always be open to you and I'll give you whatever help I can. Furthermore, I will speak to all of your other professors knowing that they will pledge the same as I have. Just do your part and you can get through this." I never forgot his kindness and encouragement. What a privilege it was to have him visit us years later in Hong Kong and we had the added privilege of visiting him and his wife in the Philippines.

We had what I consider to be an all-star cast for teachers during our time at PUC. I had Carl Coffman for Homiletics and Pastoral Training. Interestingly, the last church he pastored was in Napa, California and now I have been at that church for more than ten years. I never would have dreamed of that then. I had Roger Coon for my Christian Beliefs class, and Robert Olson for Spirit of Prophecy. I took Greek from Neils Erik Andreason, Pauline Epistles from John Staples, and Hebrew Prophets from dear sweet Paul Quimby who taught me as much about Chinese culture as Hebrew prophets.

My one year and nine months at PUC was pretty hectic to say the least. I was taking a very full academic load that consisted mainly of religion and theology classes. I did have to update a few other subjects to meet the requirements. In between and after classes I worked at the College Market and then for the evenings I got a job with a janitorial service cleaning four branches of Bank of America. Yes, I had moved up from management trainee to janitor. The good news was that the pay was more!

Every night, or sometimes very early in the morning, Ingrid and I would clean the bank in Angwin and then drive to Napa, where we cleaned two more branches and finally on to Vallejo to clean one more. We did that six nights a week for over a year. Most often we started out about 7 pm and took the children with us. The boys would help us in the first two banks and then sleep. This all involved driving a hundred miles each evening as well as the cleaning work and we would get home around midnight. It got even more complicated when our daughter Julie was born in January of '73 and Ingrid could be seen with the baby on one hip and a vacuum cleaner in the other hand. Do you have any idea how glad we were to be done with that scenario? But, we were thankful to God for it because it paid for most of our schooling.

Just to keep things interesting I also was able to be the Student Pastor for the Clearlake Church and this involved preaching every other week. Obviously our time at PUC was busy, but you know what? We had a lot of fun during that time. We didn't have any money, but neither did any of our friends. There was a whole group of us that were older and had families and we would get together and just have fun with whatever we could throw together. It was like one big family.

Early in 1973 the interviews were held for that year's graduates and I was extremely intimidated. I had doubts as to whether I would compare favorably to the other graduates and I was also pretty sure that I didn't want to get swallowed up in the realm of the large California conferences. On top of that I was hoping to get picked up by a smaller conference that would not require me to go to seminary. I knew I would benefit greatly from the educational experience, but I didn't have any idea how we would survive financially. So, I didn't sign up for any interviews. Instead I sent my name off to the Iowa Conference, which had picked up PUC students from the past because they liked the training that Elder Coffman provided. I was elated, just a few weeks later, when I received an official call from Iowa. That came before the other students had their calls from California.

On one weekend, when we were visiting back up in Ukiah, the Northern California Conference President, Helmet Retzer, was in attendance. The folks there in Ukiah were proud of their "home-grown" student and introduced me to Elder Retzer. He said, "I don't remember you from the interviews."

I replied, "I didn't interview."

"But," he said, "What if God wants you in Northern California?"

"Then I guess you'd give me a call without an interview," I said.

I don't think I handled that very well. But I believe I was where God wanted me to be.

Now it was September. I had finished Summer Quarter and had three more classes to take in order to graduate and none of them were Religion classes. I was due to begin in Iowa in January. I happened to be in conversation with the Academic Dean, Howard Hardcastle, and he asked me how things were going and I shared my schedule and plans. He told me to contact Iowa and see if I couldn't start there earlier and take the three classes through Home Study. I called Iowa and they agreed and I was a very excited young man when I shared the news with Ingrid that we could get off this crazy merry-go-round of work and begin ministry. We packed our belongings into a Ryder truck and headed east in early October.

We invited Ingrid's mom, Hanna, to move back with us and help with the children and she agreed to sign on for the adventure. Thirty-seven years later she is still with us, and what a blessing she has been. Her adventure along the way is another story all by itself!

We spent three days and two nights traveling back with Ingrid driving the station wagon and I drove the truck with one or both of the boys with me. We were all excited about going places we had never been and about starting ministry. About a hundred miles west of Des Moines, IA we had a problem. The truck started to shake badly and I eased off to the side of the highway. Upon inspection I discovered that the left rear wheel had popped off seven out of the eight lug nuts holding it on. We called Ryder and they put us in touch with a service station just a few miles ahead. We inched our way along the shoulder of I-80 and when we met with the mechanic he was amazed. He said, "There is no way that one lug nut could hold that wheel on when the other seven popped off. I can't imagine how that happened."

"Well." I said, "I know exactly how that happened and I shared just a bit of our story." I don't know if he accepted that or not, but at least he heard it! God gave us one more reason to believe that we were in His plan.

Now we faced another challenge. We were to begin our internship in Davenport, Iowa on the eastern border along the Mississippi River. However, since we were three months earlier than they had planned there was not a place for us. So, they told us to have Ingrid and the family go on to Davenport and find a rental and I was to stay in Nevada (Ne VAY duh), Iowa, where Oak Park Academy was located, and help with a series of evangelistic meetings that was just getting underway.

We got a house and got unloaded and I took off for my assignment. Somehow we managed to buy a second car and we went on like we knew what we were doing. The problem was that we didn't! Through the rest of October and all of November and December I lived in the Boy's Dorm at Oak Park. Every other weekend I could go home after church and come back on Monday. On the alternate weekends Ingrid, her mom, and the three children would come to Nevada. The only housing provided was an empty house with no furniture and mattresses on the floor that smelled strongly of mothballs. There also was no heat in the house! To make matters worse, the heater in the car didn't work right since it was set up for California and Ingrid would drive with a blanket over the steering wheel to keep warm. I don't know why I didn't ask the conference for permission to get a motel on those weekends, but we were young and just glad to be in ministry and didn't want to do something wrong. These were hard months.

I worked with the evangelist, Art Swinson, for the first five or six weeks. That provided me with some valuable experience in visitation and behind the scenes work in evangelism. We worked hard at visitation every day and then had the meetings five nights a week. I am still thankful for the things I learned working with Art.

At the close of the meetings the pastor in Nevada moved out of state. Evidently the conference was not aware of this upcoming move much, if any, in advance and my next assignment was to stay put and provide pastoral care for the church until a replacement moved in. Well, here I was with exactly two years of Adventist membership behind me and a whole six weeks of experience and I was to be the only pastor for this 350 member church. That was just a little bit intimidating, and then the real fun began.

The first real challenge I faced was that the treasurer left town and apparently took some of the funds along. If I recall correctly the church was left with over $60,000 of debt to local businesses that they thought had been paid. Now what do I do? The only thing I could think of was to call a church business meeting and lay it on the line. I then announced that we were going to take an offering to collect funds and pledges that would be paid within sixty days.

We passed the plates and tallied up the results and came up with just under half of the amount needed. So, I reported the findings and said that we needed to do that again. We passed the plates and counted once more and we were still nearly $20,000 short, which as you look at it is really pretty good. One of the local leaders was talking to the group and a man sitting toward the back of the church motioned for me to come over to him. This was a man who had left the church as a teenager and we had just baptized him in the evangelistic meetings. He lived alone in a small simple house in town and obviously had never spent money on himself. He didn't even own a car, but rode everywhere on a bicycle. He then asked me how much we were short. I told him we still needed almost $20,000 and he told me to come and see him in the morning and he would give me a check for that amount. I was one pretty excited young pastor!

My second challenge, which seemed even greater than the first, was that one dear member had the audacity to die during this time. I had prepared one funeral sermon as an assignment for Homiletics, but had zero experience as to what needed to be done or how to do it. On top of that a blizzard had hit and there was ice and snow everywhere and I was driving an old 1965 Mustang with tires that had seen better days. I went to visit with the woman whose husband had passed away and, of course, her driveway was up a hill, but I managed to get there. By the time the service was ready to begin I believe I would have gladly changed places with the deceased. These were indeed exciting times of trial by fire.

Finally, just after the first of the year, a new pastor came to town and I was able to move back to Davenport and reunite with the rest of the family. While Davenport was the church I was to have my internship in I was also primarily responsible for the church in Dubuque, Iowa, which was about 70 miles north. I preached there almost every week. I think I attended church in Davenport just three or four times and I was also called away to work another series with Art Swinson, this time in Ottumwa, Iowa. That was a lot of activity for the eight months of my internship.

Then it was time to move again. We had already moved from California to the rental house and then to the parsonage when it became available in January and now we were moving to our first district of Ames, Boone, and Perry, where we would move into a townhouse for three months until the parsonage became available. That's a lot of moves for the first year of ministry!

At last we were in our first pastorate on our own. Ames, Iowa was the primary church in our district, located about thirty miles north of Des Moines, and is the home of Iowa State University, a very beautiful campus. We were very excited about the possibilities, and having worked with the conference evangelist through two series and having conducted one of my own (with one baptism) in Dubuque, we were very anxious to have some evangelistic meetings here.

We soon discovered that there had not been any evangelism done here in many years and there had not been any baptisms in recent years as well. In fact, although the church was built as an Adventist Church, there was no baptistery in the facility.

When I announced plans for an evangelist to come and work with us I got a call from my Head Elder and he invited me to come and visit with him and another elder. They picked me up in a beautiful Cadillac and I got into the back seat and we went for a ride. They explained to me that evangelism was not the method of choice for this church to gain new members. Rather, they, and select others, were always looking for suitable members from other Adventist churches and would encourage them to transfer, thereby controlling the quality of the makeup of the church. I listened and finally responded that while I welcomed the transfer of others who wished to unite with what we were doing in Ames I also fully intended to do evangelism to reach the general population of the city. They encouraged me to think about it and took me home.

At our next church board meeting, which was only my second board meeting, I confirmed my intention of having G.D. O'Brian come to conduct meetings in about three months. The immediate reaction must have been pre-planned. My Head Elder, the other elder, the Church Clerk, the Church Treasurer, the Lay Activities Leader and the Sabbath School Superintendant all stood up and announced that they were leaving and would be transferring to other churches. On his way out the door the exact words of my head elder were, "Without me and my money this church will fall flat on its face." I replied, "You said that to the wrong pastor," and I turned to the three board members who remained and broke down and wept.

Was I frightened? You bet I was. I didn't know what I was doing. I didn't know what the Conference President would think because I knew this man was a man of influence. But, I also knew that God had called us to do more than invite "quality" persons to transfer their membership. The end result was that our church of 100 members was now a church of 60 members and I had accomplished that pretty much single handedly in a matter of two months. Not bad huh? Perhaps having a "remnant" of 60% isn't really all that bad.

The remaining members were not only willing to carry on, but they were excited. For the first time in many years they felt like we had a chance to do something and be involved in outreach. To start things off we rented the building previously occupied by JC Penney's in downtown Ames. Next we turned that empty space into a sanctuary with temporary walls, curtains and other decorations. We got the lumber donated by the local lumberyard with the understanding that we would return it when done. Our men even repaired the broken heating system and finished that just prior to the first night's meeting. We brought in a portable baptistery and the place looked pretty fantastic. At the close of the meetings we baptized fourteen precious new members into the Ames Church. Following those meetings we raised the money and had a baptistery built into the church and by the end of the year our membership was almost back up to the 100 mark again. That was a precious lesson to me that God can do anything if we will just give Him a chance!

There were many other wonderful times and experiences in that first district. We did evangelism in all of the churches and we ingathered funds for disaster relief in each town as well. Now, more than 35 years later we still have ongoing friendships with the people from that short time that we were there. After a year and a half the conference moved us to Sioux City and we had the little church in Hawarden as well.

The Conference leadership told us that they wanted to purchase a parsonage in Sioux City, but that we should plan to move into a temporary rental first. We told them that we had done that twice already and we plead with them to purchase the house right away. Bless their hearts, they had the Treasurer, Bob Rawson, go with us and we got to help pick out the house, which was right down the street from the church. Sioux City was another short stay, but we had some wonderful experiences there as well. In fact we managed to have a baptism every month during the fifteen months that we pastored there. Again, many of those dear people remain friends with us today.

Well, that was a lot to happen in the third decade of life. In that ten year period I went from being a two pack a day smoker and an alcoholic, through several jobs and one marriage, into a new marriage and joining the Adventist Church, preparing for ministry and ending the decade with four years of pastoral ministry under our belts. The next decade would bring new kinds of experiences and excitement. We'll get to that in chapter eight!

Chapter the Seventh

The Fourth Week

OK, the party was over and I needed to get back on the road. There was definitely something exciting about actually heading west. I knew I was going home! It was certainly hard this morning to leave Ingrid again. I would miss a really fun day with her and our daughter as well, but now it would be actually less than three weeks until we would be together again. So, I was up early because today was going to be a really big day with lots of miles and three interviews. It is also a good thing I didn't know what was in store for me later in the week!

From Inwood, WV, where our son-in-law's parents, Norm and Carol Wootton, live I headed up into Pennsylvania and west toward Pittsburg. This is a very pretty part of the country. Riding through the countryside of the Appalachian Mountains brings a series of beautiful scenes.

At my first gas stop I met a fellow rider and we started chatting. Of course he wanted to know where I was headed, which is the common way of getting conversations going with another biker. When I explained the course already covered and where I was headed he just looked at me and I have never seen such a look of envy in all my life. He was almost moved to tears at the prospect. And when I told him it was on full salary while doing this he was totally awestruck. I think it was then that it fully sunk in as to how blessed I really was. I was having a motorcycle trip of a lifetime, getting paid for it, and hadn't had one mishap or really difficult day. There wasn't much time to chat so I just saddled up and left him shaking his head and coveting.

The turnpikes in Pennsylvania are a real pain. Any time you have to come up with exact change on a bike, it is a challenge. Gloves have to come off and pockets have to be dug into. Inevitably something will drop and I can sense the rolling of the eyes from the car behind. I wish they would just issue value tickets, like on the subway systems, and I could simply purchase enough to get me through and insert the card at each entry and exit. But, I made it through and rode into Carnegie, PA some three and a half hours and 200 miles later. It was about 10:30 in the morning.

CARNEGIE, PENNSYLVANIA

I had spoken with Andy Clarke, who was heading up this unique inner city work, over the weeks leading up to today and I knew that he was not going to be able to meet with me, as he would be out of town. I was looking for the Conscious Café and was having just a moment of difficulty determining just where it was located when a young man across the street asked me what I was looking for. I told him and he said, "You must be Marvin." Well, Andy had changed his plans and I am so glad he did because nobody else could have given me the story of the miracle that had taken place in this Pittsburg suburb.

Take a former drug dealer and $500 a day addict, add a full measure of Jesus into his life, immerse him in a college curriculum focused on inner city ministry, mix a bold step from the Pennsylvania Conference President, turn up the heat and take out a wonderfully successful Adventist church planter. Nothing is too big for God!

I read the sign above his desk as we sat and talked. It says, "I choose to follow the road less traveled…Now where the heck am I?" Well, Andy knows exactly where he is. He is precisely where God put him. How else could you possibly explain this story?

In September of 2004 Hurricanes Frances and Ivan slammed into this Pittsburg suburb and homes were flooded everywhere. Adventist Community Services was called in and ministered to a large number of families. Ray Hartwell, President of the Pennsylvania Conference, saw an opportunity to do more than just fix homes and led in extending the opportunity for Andy and his wife, Mayda, to come and go to work.

Carnegie, Pennsylvania had the least SDA presence of any of the 25 largest metropolitan areas in the U.S. It also had the most churches, bars, and funeral homes per capita. They were happy to receive help, but they did not want another church. So, Andy did not work on building a church. Instead he worked on building relationships.

The job description from the conference was three fold:

1. Follow God's leading as laid out in Ministry of Healing p. 143.
2. Keep the conference informed on progress and intentionality.
3. Build a group of people who desire to worship and grow.

You have to take those in the right order. MH, page 143 offers this: ***"Christ's method alone will give true success in reaching the people. The Saviour mingled with men as one who desired their good. He showed His sympathy for them, ministered to their needs, and won their confidence. Then He bade them, 'Follow Me.'"*** That takes time.

Andy began building relationships in the community and drawing people together with the purpose of rebuilding many of the homes in the area. He drove me past home after home that his army of volunteers had refurbished. This was a totally interdenominational effort. In a short time he became the President of the local Ministerial Association with 26 different denominations working together.

Gradually he gathered funding and support that allowed him to add staff and to open a variety of social services including tutoring, counseling and other needs. The work was clearly growing, as was the trust of the community. In December of 2006 the enterprise applied for an occupancy permit so that they could hold worship services. The City Council was strongly opposed to this move. They told Andy, "We love your work and all that you are providing, but we have more churches than we need now and we won't be approving another one." Andy asked for the item to be placed on the agenda anyway. They were going to have to officially turn him down.

Usually no more than a dozen citizens turn out for City Council Meetings. They are pretty boring entertainment. However, in this case more than 200 showed up. One by one the various ministers, priests, and rabbis presented their support for the Adventists. The theater owner and other business owners made their appeal. ***Residents of all ages spoke up and finally there was the clincher. One of the local bar owners stood before the council and told how the Adventists had ministered to and helped her daughter. Then she said, "And you will approve this request because I give all of you free drinks every Friday night!" I don't know of another SDA Church that got started on testimony like that, but I love it!***

Today PULSE (People United by Love to Serve and Empower) Community Fellowship is a rapidly expanding ministry. I recently saw that they were looking for a full time Pastor to work with them. ***They had their first two baptisms just two weeks after I was there, on July 18, 2009, and they had six more preparing. To be baptized in the PULSE church you must have an understanding of God, understand the fundamental beliefs of the Adventist faith, and be involved in the ministry to the Carnegie community.***

Can you tell that I was excited, inspired, and energized by my all too short visit with Andy? ***This is absolutely what I was looking for on my journey. I had already seen a great deal of creativity and "outside the box" thinking and some of it was very effective in reaching new people. Here I saw raw energy, faith, and commitment that was truly unique. That is not intended to lift this ministry above others or to say that this is the way anyone else should do it. However, if this level of energy, faith, and commitment were duplicated anywhere, including in my own ministry, it would be inevitable that miracles would happen.***

Now I needed to move on to my next destination of Newark, Ohio, which was another 150 miles west on I-70. Today I was glad for Interstate riding just because I had so many miles to cover. I would still have another 120 miles after this visit to get to my evening destination. Thank God the weather was good!

NEWARK, OHIO

The Newark, Ohio Church is not remarkable in itself. It has a nice facility that is definitely rural, but they have a strong community service presence and a thrift store on Main Street. They have done many outreach programs and Pastor Tom Hughes was doing evangelism in the Fall.

Probably the biggest challenge here is that the average age of the church membership is about 70. Don't get me wrong; there is nothing bad about 70 year old church members. We have lots of them in our church too and I'm not too far from joining them, but when that is your average age it's going to be hard to keep going, let alone grow.

The members are doing what they can to reach young families. They have a big VBS program. They do have a school, but it has only one teacher and about ten students. One of the elders is a full time chaplain at a nearby hospital and they are a friendly group.

One unique outreach, and probably my primary reason for stopping here, is that Pr. Tom is quite a biker. He is a chaplain for a national motorcycle group and has written a special edition of Steps to Christ entitled "Biker Steps to Jesus". He also has written a set of "Biker Bible Studies." Unfortunately Tom was out of town and I didn't get to meet with him personally. Like I said, the biggest challenge is going to be to integrate the bikers and other young families with an aging church body. It can be done, but it is going to require some give and take for sure.

Back on my trusty steed I now headed west once more, picking up I-71 once I was on the south side of Columbus, Ohio. I was enjoying the visits immensely, but I have to admit that the riding was less than exhilarating. I was definitely in the "git 'er done" frame of mind. There just have to be days like that when you're covering 12,000 miles in six weeks of riding and making at least two visits on most days. So, just keep your eyes on the road, the rest of the drivers, and the highway signs.

MONTE SAHLIN

My final destination for the day was Springboro, Ohio and the home of Monte Sahlin and his gracious wife, Norma. It was getting late, but they waited dinner for me and we had a marvelous picnic dinner in the back yard with his daughter and son-in-law, who are also in ministry and doing some very interesting things.

Monte is widely recognized as the North American Division's statistics guru and evaluator of trend,s among his many other gifts. He took me down into his "office" which takes up pretty much the entire basement and boasts a library of many thousands of books. To make it even more daunting is the fact that he's read most of them.

We talked late into the night about the trip, the project, other studies being done that would parallel this and a variety of other things. I always have enjoyed Monte's company and insights, but to share it in his own home was indeed a special treat.

A morning breakfast and I was on the road again, as the song says. Today would be a bit easier with my first stop being in Dayton. This was easy as we're only talking about 170 miles. I was wishing there could be a stop also in Kettering, which was just off the highway, but my appointments were set. That was the continuing frustration of the schedule I had set. I wish, in many ways, that I could have taken the entire three months of Sabbatical to do this and allow for more stops and more flexibility. However, this was already hard enough on my sweet wife and it probably wouldn't have made the outcome and general consensus of the book any different. It would have given more examples of what is happening in other growing churches, but you can always do a little research on your own.

TOLEDO, OHIO

The Toledo First Seventh-day Adventist Church is a very beautiful facility and very well kept. Once I arrived I met Mike Fortune, who has been the pastor there for the past two years, and certainly keeps in touch with the times and is on the cutting edge of outreach possibilities. Interestingly, when I pastored in Vienna, VA I followed Mike's dad, John, who pastored there fore several years.

Once again, as we look at the opportunity to grow a church, both spiritually and numerically, we have to be willing to change and to try new things. ***Mike handed me a sheet of potential outreach strategies that he and his church leaders had brainstormed. They then picked three of the items to focus on. You can't do everything at once and do it well. But once they started something it was not set in concrete. If it worked, they would keep it. If not, try something else.*** I loved the statement at the bottom of his list:

"According to the Adventist Church's Center for Creative Ministry (we actually have one!!!) the median age of an Adventist American is 52 while the median age of the average American is 35. But another reason people in the church need to be innovating inside and outside is because, according to The Barna Group, 71% of those average Americans won't be attending church on any day this weekend. The good news, I suppose if there is some, is that 78% of those unchurched Americans are willing to have a spiritual conversation. They just aren't willing to have it in church now, or maybe ever."

Mike states that through continuing contact with a number of creative pastors who are reaching that 71% he stays encouraged and so do the leaders in Toledo First as they keep trying to reach this continuously growing mission field where they live.

What kinds of things are they trying at Toledo First? They have

"adopted" a local Hospice Women's Shelter and provide a number of methods of support. They have VBS on a weekly basis for ages 4-12 and they conduct it from 11:00 – 12:00 and from 5:00 – 6:00. They love to have block parties at the church and the real highlight happens on Labor Day weekend when they host a "Kidz Crazy Car Show". Last Labor Day they had fifty-two cars entered. They had concessions, face painting, and a NHRA dragster for everyone to enjoy.

Mike shared a fun story with me. At the car show he was out in the parking lot grilling hot dogs. Someone asked him why they were grilling beef hot dogs. He remarked, "Because most of these folks don't like veggie dogs!" But if they wanted veggie dogs those were available too. You have to meet the folks where they are. This event has been a huge hit in the area and is beginning to compete with the bigger car shows. Many people ask if they can see inside the church while they are there and Mike loves to show them around. The slogan that is often shared is that "God loves you like crazy!"

Toledo First is also globally focused. They host a large Valentine's Party every year to raise money for projects and mission trips to help in Rwanda and India currently. Locally they are looking for a good storefront location to do outreach off campus.

This creative congregation has three main focal points.

1. Focus on Children's Ministry.
2. Everything they do is Christ centered.
3. They believe in "SHOUTING" the Gospel.

Here again I was encouraged, impressed, and hopeful for the future of our church. There is no "status quo" or "we've always done it that way" attitude here. Building relationships, meeting needs, and inviting others to follow is what they are all about. Keep up the good work Toledo!

BATTLE CREEK, MICHIGAN

Moving on I was now headed up to a great historical site in Adventist history in the place of Battle Creek, Michigan. This is where the organized work of the denomination began. ***I knew that Battle***

Creek had a rich history. Now I wanted to know if it had a vision to the future.

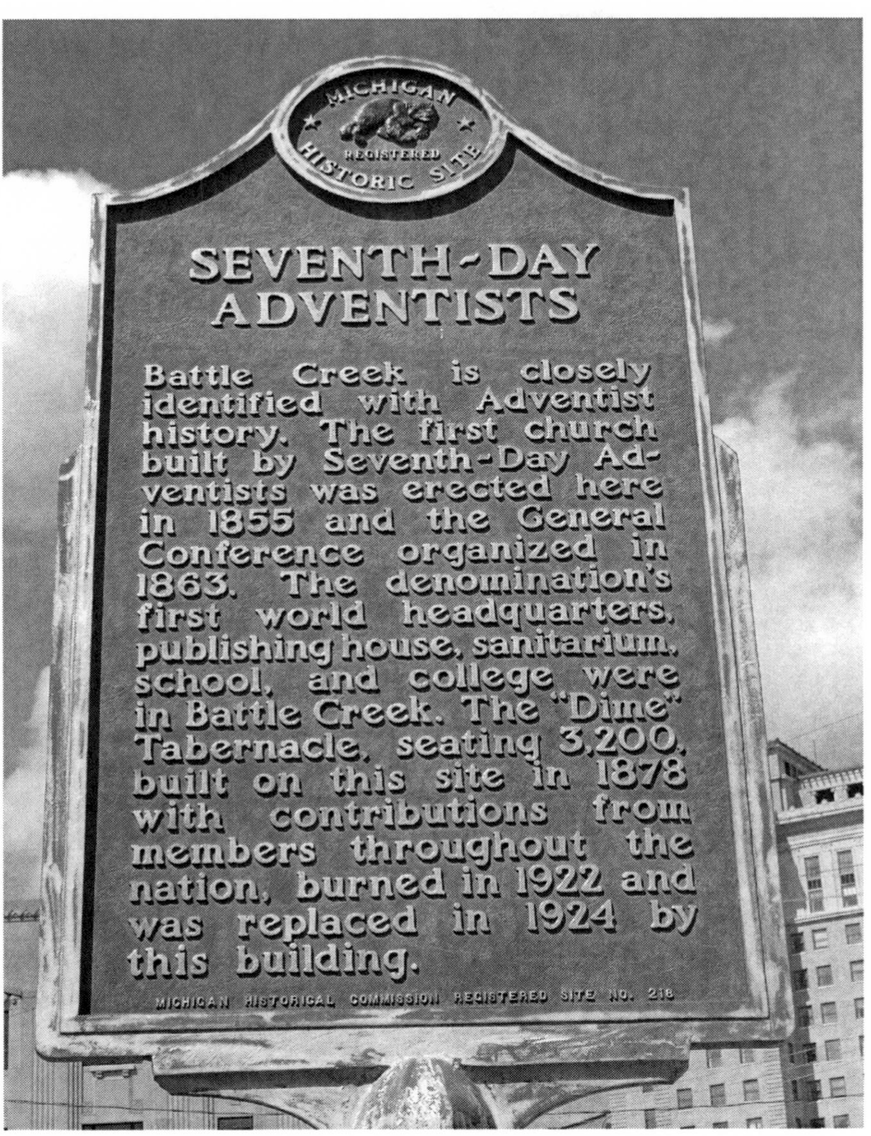

I've been here previously a few times. Just a few years ago I was privileged to be a delegate to the North American Division Annual Meetings for several sessions and one of those was held in Battle Creek rather than in Silver Spring, Maryland. I got to see some fascinating insights at the Adventist History Village there as well as many interesting buildings and memorials related to the Battle Creek Sanitarium and the Kellogg enterprises. Now I just wanted to meet with the pastor and see what was happening today.

Pr. Bruce Moore met me at the church and gave me the grand tour. This is certainly a church rich with history and the interior is stunningly beautiful. This facility was completed in 1926 to replace the well known Dime Tabernacle, which burned down in 1922. Battle Creek's first church was built in 1855 and had among its charter members names such as James and Ellen White, Uriah Smith and a host of other familiar pioneers of our work.

After spending some time walking the halls of this great building we drove over to the Oak Hill Cemetery where I once again visited the graves of James and Ellen White and many other fascinating names. Battle Creek was home to not only John Harvey Kellogg, but also his brother, W. H. Kellogg who went on to establish the great cereal giant and his major competitor C.W. Post. Sojourner Truth, the consummate voice for abolition and civil rights made her home here as well. We drove around the city and Bruce showed me several other interesting points of church historical significance.

Returning to his home for the evening and having a wonderful meal prepared by his wife, we sat and talked about the current outreach efforts of the Battle Creek Tabernacle. ***They were in the process of sending out 45,000 copies of the Great Controversy in preparation for meetings that were to be held last Fall. They also use the programming of 3ABN to a large extent to garner interests. Outreach efforts here are fairly standard with VBS, Depression Seminars and other similar programs. They also partner with the Salvation Army for food distribution and they have adopted a section of highway leading into town.***

One of their great challenges financially is the support of Battle Creek Academy. Bruce shared with me that 64% of their budget goes to the school in subsidies. In spite of that, the church family has taken on many projects in the local church, the local community and for world mission outreach. He has been the Sr. Pastor here for six years and finds the church to be very supportive.

As I left this great place with so much meaning to our denomination I was touched by its heritage and history of sacrifice. I could see that the church family is doing many things to stay in touch with and meet the needs of the community. The church is still a very strong church. I pray that they will be able to also reach the young unchurched families in the community who are not necessarily impressed with our past.

ANDREWS UNIVERSITY

The skies were looking pretty dark as I left Battle Creek on Wednesday morning and headed toward Berrien Springs, Michigan just 85 miles away. I had an appointment to meet with Joe Kidder, Professor of Church Growth at Andrews University Seminary. He has done some extensive research on growing SDA churches and I was anxious to pick his brain.

I always enjoy being on the campus of Andrews University. Although I never attended the Seminary, I did spend six weeks at the Missions Institute in preparation for our service in Hong Kong, which will be shared in the next chapter. I have also visited there a number of times and I love the international flavor and the learning opportunities that abound. So, I made my way to the Seminary Building and found that it had changed some since my last visit and it took me awhile to find Dr. Kidder's office. When I did find it I learned that he was ill and was unable to meet with me, but had left a message for me to call him at his home. We spent a delightful hour sharing information, experiences, and perceptions even though I knew he wasn't feeling all that well. I am so grateful for his kindness to me.

Dr. Kidder has been researching SDA churches across the North American Division to find those that can qualify to be called "growing churches." To meet his criteria a church must have grown by 10% or more for five consecutive years. I was interested to learn that there are only twenty-six churches that met those criteria. I was happy to learn that several of them were on my list. He is currently writing a book to talk about his findings and I will be anxious to read it.

I then went over to the Pioneer Memorial Church to see if, by chance, I might catch up with Sr. Pastor Dwight Nelson. I knew that he also was on a sabbatical to finish the daily devotional he was working on. Dwight and I pastored neighboring churches when I was in Coos Bay, Oregon and he was in Coquille and Myrtle Creek. Those were great days and we had many good times riding dirt bikes in the dunes and sharing ministry experiences together. As it turned out he was not at his office, but I did have a chance to meet with Esther Knott.

Esther was on the staff at the Sligo Church in Takoma Park, Maryland, when I was working in the Potomac Conference in the 80's and 90's and I loved her spirit and creativity. She has been at Pioneer Memorial since the mid-90's and is doing a wonderful work, primarily with small groups. We sat and talked for about an hour and just got caught up on family, friends, and the focus of our ministries. There is no doubt that, particularly in large congregations, there is no substitute for small groups where individuals can be more intimately connected for nurture and outreach. It was so much fun to see how God has led and blessed in her ministry.

After a quick walk around the campus and a visit to Chan Shun Hall to see the bust of my former church member I hopped back into the saddle and gave a nervous look to the skies. They didn't look too promising and I had a long way to go. Davenport, Iowa was my destination for the evening and I was looking forward to it because that was where I did my internship way back in 1973-74.

Before entering I-80 and heading west the rain started in and by the time many miles were covered it was pouring. I stopped and put on my rain gear for the second time on the trip and it worked very well. I had purchased the Tourmaster Sentinel jacket and the separate pants with the heat protective legs. They kept me dry and my Gore-Tex boots from Cabellas also kept my feet dry. I have to put in a plug for these boots here. From the first moment I put them on they felt like gloves on my feet. They were a gift from my son-in-law, Will Wootton and my daughter, Julie, and I love them (the kids and the boots). They were worn for three weeks in Mozambique earlier in the year, when a group from our church went on a mission trip to build a church, and every day of this bike trip, and my feet never suffered for a moment. So, while dry, that doesn't mean that I was having a good time!

Riding on the interstate for more than 200 miles in an endlessly driving rain is not high on my list of favorite things to do. The bike handled fine and I had good tires, but the spray from the trucks almost blinds you and I must have passed a few hundred of them. I forget if the speed limit there is 65 or 70. I was rolling along with traffic at just under 80, but every truck brought near blindness. I never felt unsafe, but I was certainly uncomfortable and not enjoying the ride. I got plenty of curious looks when I would stop for gas or just for a break in the concentration.

DAVENPORT, IOWA

Finally I arrived at the home of Pr. Bob and Angie Joseph. This was a home I was well familiar with since my internship was done at this church and the parsonage was the same. When I arrived I found a note on the door explaining that Bob and Angie had been suddenly called out to help a member and they would be returning in about two hours. I had just missed them. The note also suggested that there should be someone at the church and I could wait there, but I was very anxious for a warm shower so I went and checked into a nearby Comfort Inn. I just wanted to get out of these clothes and cleaned up and into something a lot more comfortable. I called them and they understood and we agreed to meet in the morning for breakfast.

A shower feels good at the end of any day of riding, but a day like today really makes it seem special. With that accomplished, a warm meal, and a Skype with Ingrid, my world was good again.

The next morning I got a good look at the bike. It was pretty discouraging in appearance from yesterday's ride. The motel had a hose hooked up outside and they gave me a few rags to use and I was able to wash away most of the grime. I hate riding a really dirty bike. It wasn't raining today and I was happy to be feeling good and looking presentable.

My breakfast meeting with Bob and Angie was delicious and delightful. We spent an hour or so just talking about the current programs in the Davenport Church. They have been there for three years now. ***I was especially intrigued by one outreach they engage in called, "Church and Rescue." I love the title. Members actually go door to door through various neighborhoods and simply ask if the residents have any prayer requests. There is no pressure and no gimmicks, just a contact and a sincere offer to pray with the people right then and there and/or to take the prayer request along and add it to a church prayer request book.*** This offers a great opportunity to check back and see how things have worked out for those who share requests. ***The Davenport Community Service Center also provides dinners periodically for emergency workers to show appreciation for the work that they do.*** The school, where both of our boys attended, now has 32 students in grades 1-9 and appears to be doing quite well.

Angie has done evangelism as well and I was told that she was the first woman to hold meetings in the Iowa/Missouri Conference. It was a lot of fun for me to return here and to see that the work is going well and some creativity is going into the outreach.

IOWA CITY, IOWA

The plan now was for me to follow Bob to the Iowa City Church for an area pastor's meeting. This gave me a good chance to visit with a number of pastors to get a feel for how things are working in this Mid-American conference. I met with Bob from Davenport, Mark Luckiesh from Waterloo and Dubuque (Dubuque was where I held my first evangelistic series which resulted in one baptism), Roy Weeden from Mason City, Hampton, and Charles City, Gary Birth from Hawkeye, Waukon, and Dave Bissell from Cedar Rapids.

I heard pretty much what I would have expected to hear from this group. The work is hard and the members are not often excited about "new and creative" methods. ***One of the great blessings and sources of encouragement for these dedicated men is the opportunity to meet and share and pray together.*** It was a privilege to sit with them for a couple of hours. I was reminded of how fortunate I was currently to be pastoring in a beautiful part of northern California with a very supportive and active large congregation that embraces new thoughts and to have two very creative associates. I remember well the early days of ministry with multiple churches spread far apart and just trying to meet the church needs, let alone explore creative options. ***These men all work hard and are very dedicated to their ministry and their churches. It was refreshing to see that God has so many faithful servants everywhere I traveled.***

AMES, IOWA

I left Iowa City now and headed west to Ames, Iowa, home of Iowa State University. My hostess for the evening was going to be Treva Martsching. Treva was my Church Clerk when I came to Ames way back in 1974. Her husband, Bill, who has since passed away, was my Head Deacon and these two were a vital part of the backbone of that church. This precious lady, nearly ninety years old, still cares for children with disabilities. She was doing that when I first met her and she has continued through all the years. The love that she gives to these precious infants and toddlers is amazing. What fun it was going to be to reminisce about the past and to talk about the future.

I knew how to find the house without looking at any maps and it looked pretty much the same. The church also looked the same and that is not necessarily a good thing. The members have done a good job in keeping the property neat, but the church is old, small, and not suited to growth in this town hosting a major university. I am convinced that not infrequently if a church wants to grow they will need to either relocate or begin a second group that meets in a new location. Certainly this would be the case in Ames.

Pastor Jody Dickhaut, who also pastors the Ankeny Church, was not able to meet with me, but he graciously allowed me to meet with David Lincoln. Dave is currently working in the Trust Department for the Iowa/Missouri Conference, but he pastored the Ames Church for about ten years. Obviously we spent some time swapping stories and going back over some of the church history, but we also talked about the church's potential.

When I came to this district Ames was the principal church. Now it is the much smaller "little sister" to the Ankeny congregation. One still has to recognize, however, that the potential here is enormous with the university

presence. However, to reach this potential is going to require totally new methods and approaches to ministry. I believe it could be very exciting for the right group to open up a whole new Adventist presence here.

It is interesting to note that even after having left here some thirty-four years ago I still feel like, to a certain extent, this is my church family. I think every pastor must feel that to one degree or another about every church they have served. This was a marvelous place for us to begin ministry and I thank God for this group of saints and their patience in working with a young pastor who had only nine months of pastoral experience and three years of Adventist background. There must be a special reward in heaven for congregations like this.

Friday dawned and I had my next appointment in Sioux City, Iowa. This is where I pastored after the conference moved us from Ames after just a year and a half. The weather was looking a little concerning and so I got up early and left quietly even before Treva got up. Filling up with gas and heading up I-35 I would go west on state highway 20. This is a ride of about 185 miles, but I knew the road and remembered that it wasn't all high-speed travel.

When I got to Hwy 20 and started heading west it began to appear that I could be in for an "interesting" ride. I stopped and put on my rain jacket and decided against the hassle of getting the pants on over my boots unless I was actually going to hit some heavy weather. That turned out to be a very big mistake. I was watching a massive dark, no make that black, sky up ahead and was just starting to look for a place to safely pull over and get the rest of my rain gear on when the full force of the storm hit with stunning speed.

This was country highway and there were not many places to pull over and not much shoulder either. The real problem was that I was almost instantly reduced to near blindness. I have never seen a storm this fierce and moving this fast, and was now in the midst of it with nowhere to go. The concave form of my seat quickly filled with water and it was way too late for raingear even if I could have stopped.

The speed limit here was 55, but I couldn't see to go faster than 20 as visibility was reduced to about 30 feet. There were many big rig trucks coming the opposite direction adding more wind and sheets of extra water to my challenges. They were reduced to about the same speed, but I couldn't help wonder if there might be someone coming up behind me going twice my speed and not enough visibility to see me in time. I have to tell you that for the first time in my life of riding bikes real fear had entered the picture and I started to pray out loud.

This went on for about ten minutes when the lightning was no longer distant. Lightning was now striking on both sides of the highway and here I was sitting on a metal tank filled with gas. Accounts where bikes had been hit with lightning were not unfamiliar to me and I knew the outcome of that was not good other than the fact that I would get to meet Jesus sooner than expected.

There was absolutely no choice but to keep moving forward and praying. There are no bridges or overpasses along here. There is an occasional farm, but I couldn't see where to pull off and wasn't sure that sitting in a farmer's driveway was any safer. Besides, by keeping moving I would get through it sooner. It was a full twenty-five minutes after this ordeal started when Sac City came into view just as I was reaching the edge of this massive storm. Stopping at the first gas station/convenience store I was thankful for the covered pump area. As I began to get off the bike to consider my options, six people from inside the store came out and stood around me. One of them said, "Tell me you didn't just ride through that!" I replied that there really weren't any choices. They told me that was the worst thunderstorm they had ever seen in those parts and they were all waiting it out to even venture out in their cars. Visibly shaken I took a few minutes to just talk it out and share with them the fact that I had not been riding alone.

SIOUX CITY, IOWA

Now late for my next appointment I called the church in Sioux City and was able to let them know about my delay and they said there was a good group of my former members there and they would wait for me. I didn't bother to change, but just filled up again and kept on riding, thankful for the blue patches I was seeing up ahead.

It helped to not have to consult directions to find the church. I easily found Aspenwood Street and rode up past the parsonage where we used to live and pulled into the church parking lot at the top of the hill. There in the Fellowship Hall were a dozen or more of my church family and it was very good to see them. It had been more than thirty years since we pastored there, but I was still able to call many of them by name. Some had changed a lot and others not so much. They just smiled and shook their heads as their former pastor puddled into the room and then they laughed as I pulled off my gloves to reveal completely black hands due to the wet black leather. My trip to the men's room to see what I could do to alter the picture was a pretty hopeless venture. I was thankful for the donuts and drinks that they had brought and we just started to share together.

The Sioux City Church has not exactly flourished through the past three decades. The facility is quite attractive and is in a wonderful hilltop location. ***They run a fruit program here that has done very well and does put them in contact with a large number of people from the community,*** but I don't know how much effective follow-up has been done. I do know that evangelism in many of these mid-western places is hard. Most people are part of families with long standing traditions and change does not come easily.

I was, however, very impressed with one new program they had begun. They have a schoolteacher that began a tutoring program for students in the area that the church offers absolutely free. I give them major kudos for this innovative idea and believe that this could be the start of some relationships that could bear real "fruit."

Like so many churches in our denomination the congregation in Sioux City is aging and they are going to have to make adaptations to the needs and thinking of younger families if they want to have a real future. There is absolutely nothing wrong with the people that make up the church. They have hearts of gold, but what brought them into the church is not likely to bring in the current generation of young families.

After an hour and a half of visiting, my jeans were dry so there wasn't much point in changing now. I got back on the bike and headed south down I-29 and then over to Lincoln, Nebraska for the Sabbath. You can bet I was keeping a nervous eye on the skies in every direction. There was no desire to repeat the morning's ride. As it turned out it was a very pleasant 160 mile trip and I arrived at the lovely home of Rocky and Darla Peterson.

LINCOLN, NEBRASKA

Darla and our family go way back to that first church in Ames, Iowa where her family was a vital part of the church. Darla used to babysit for our daughter and we even took her along on a trip to California. It has been so much fun to watch through the years as she and Rocky raised a group of four precious daughters of their own. She got all the practice from us!

It was so nice to have this Friday night in the home of friends. It was also nice to be there early enough to do some much needed laundry! While the clothes were washing I did a little cleaning of my own, but the black hands were not going easily! I also managed to do another cleaning on the bike and we were all ready for Sabbath.

Darla and Rocky are very involved in the College View Church. Churches that are part of our institutions have a life of their own. They are valuable bodies of believers, but they don't face the same challenges as other church families so ***I opted to go to a newer church plant on the outskirts of Lincoln called New Creation.*** They meet in a storefront location. They had to move recently because the previous storefront became too small. Nice problem, huh?

NEW CREATION FELLOWSHIP

I parked the bike and walked in the front doors and was immediately greeted with a smile and a hug, handed a lesson quarterly, and led over to the refreshment center for hot drinks, cold drinks, and pastries. Yes, I did feel welcome!

As I see it, there is certainly a lot of controversy in churches today over worship style, music, and what is and is not appropriate for reverence in worship. I have lived in Asia for six years and have traveled and preached fairly extensively throughout the world. There are surely huge differences in worship style, music, and traditions in various countries and cultures. What is accepted and expected depends very much on the culture that surrounds you. We certainly have some varied cultural (temperament) variations right here in the good old USA! Personally, I can totally enjoy a very formal, "high" church format with pipe organ, hymns, and a lot of structure to the order of service. I can also embrace a very relaxed, informal service with music that is contemporary. Yes, I do have some parameters as to what I really enjoy and I want to worship regularly in a format that meets my spiritual needs, but that doesn't make other formats wrong.

What I tend to like about churches like New Creation is the absolute

sense of love and welcome that is extended. I am free to get a cup of coffee or not. I am free to stand during praise songs or not. I can wear a suit, slacks and sport shirt, jeans and T-shirt, or biker clothes and not be judged or shunned.

I love to sing any kind of hymn or praise song that is sung with joy and enthusiasm. Far too often I have sat in churches and a beautiful hymn is sung with such lack of feeling and monotony that I prayed a prayer of apology to God for the "noise" that was coming His way. On the other hand, I recall sitting in the Rose Bowl in Pasadena, California with 55,000 men at a Promise Keeper's weekend and singing "A Mighty Fortress Is Our God" and it brought tears to my eyes and my heart was deeply moved.

What I tend to like, and see more of at less formal, more contemporary services, is joy! I see and sense and feel joy and freedom and a very warm sense of instant belonging. We have tried to bring that into our church in Napa, which is actually fairly traditional, even though many other nearby congregations don't think so. We have a praise team at least twice a month. We used to have a team with electric guitars, the full drums (which seems to be the real dividing point in worship comfort) and then on alternate weeks we have an orchestra (which I sometimes conduct by the way) and pipe organ. I sometimes joke that we are equal opportunity offenders.

New Creation was a delightful worship experience. A marvelous young lady, Tanya Cochran, gave the message, "King of Pop, King of Kings", and compared the followers (worshippers) of the late Michael Jackson to those who profess the King of Kings. It was timely and thought provoking, relevant and worshipful. After church I was invited to join a group for lunch before heading further west. Thank you, New Creation, for a wonderful Sabbath experience!

Now I had the rest of the afternoon to get as far west through Nebraska as I could, which turned out to be Ogallala, Nebraska, some 280 miles away. I stopped there and enjoyed a good rest after a full and wonderful Sabbath. As always, I checked the weather report and looked at the potential thunderstorms in northern Colorado, especially close to the Rockies. That was exactly where I would be tomorrow night.

Chapter the Eighth

The Fourth Decade

One afternoon in the Spring of 1977, while sitting in my basement office at the parsonage in Sioux City, Iowa, I received a phone call from Jack Harris, President of the Oregon Conference. Wow, this was a new experience for me. I had never put my name out for a move and was totally caught off guard by the conversation. He asked if I would have any interest in pastoring in the Oregon Conference. I told him that the West Coast was home to me and that we had a lot of family from both sides in Washington and California and that we would be interested. He arranged to stop in Sioux City on his flight home from back east and we met him in the airport and had a good visit.

The result was that we moved after just over a year in Sioux City. This did not set well with the church or with the conference leadership. I admit that the time in Sioux City was too short, however the conference had a habit of moving young pastors way too quickly anyway. The conference was not happy because I was not yet ordained, and thus not really eligible to receive a call to another conference, but they did not block it and we did move to Coos Bay, Oregon.

This was a good move for us in many ways. It was nice to be closer to family. Too many times we had left Iowa at 6 pm and driven 36 hours straight through to maximize our time during a short vacation. Coos Bay was also a great place to live and pastor. We enjoyed our church family so much. In fact, one of my members from there is now my member again in Napa! We were getting involved in community ministry. I had a weekly radio program and the church was looking forward to soon building their new sanctuary.

Then it happened again! We were sitting down to dinner one evening when the phone rang. I took the call in my home office and found myself speaking to Don Roth, who was the liaison between the General Conference and the Far Eastern Division. The question this time was, "Would you have any interest in pastoring the English speaking church in Hong Kong?"

"What in the world?"

"What kind of a question was that?"

"Who put my name in for that?"

"Can we have a few days to talk about this?"

Well, we talked for a bit and, of course, I could have time to think and pray it through. I went back to the dinner table. They had heard parts of the conversation and, obviously, this changed our dinner conversation a great deal. One of the first things we did was to grab an atlas to find out exactly where Hong Kong was located!

How do you process something like this? I certainly had no clue. We did find out how they got my name. It seems that Roger Coon, who had been one of my professors at PUC and now was the Director of the Ellen G. White Estate, had passed by Don Roth at the Sligo Church and Don asked Roger if he had any names to suggest for this post. I had recently seen Dr. Coon at the Southern Oregon Campmeeting and my name was fresh in his mind and he thought that we might be a good match for this mission opportunity.

Well, we talked about it as a family. We had never considered mission service, but we all began to get just a little bit excited about the adventure and experience that was being held out to us. We called Don Roth back and told him that we would like to have a week to test the waters and pray. That was fine with him. Next we contacted our realtor and put the house on the market. The next day the house sold for the full asking price. Our decision was made for us! We were headed to Hong Kong after just two years in Coos Bay and only six years of ministry experience. I surely was hoping that God knew what He was doing.

Things were really in a blur now. Phone calls and documents were going back and forth to Washington, D.C. Our family that we had moved to Oregon to be closer to were wondering what they had done to cause us to move so far away. We had to not only pack, but also keep in mind we were packing for an overseas move. We ended up selling most of our belongings. Everything that we took had to be labeled, listed, priced as to replacement value, and packed securely. Passports had to be obtained and shots had to be administered. Oh, that was fun! I promised the kids that if they didn't cry until after the shots were given that we'd all go get a Peanut Buster Parfait from Dairy Queen. They made it just fine. I started a Five-day Stop Smoking Plan that evening and got so sick I had to cancel it and send them all home! Our daughter, Julie, who was five at the time, played the nurse that evening and kept bringing cold washcloths to the rest of us who were so sick.

Next stop was Andrews University for six weeks of Missions Institute. This was a fabulous and very valuable experience for the whole family. We made so many precious friends among other missionaries going to all parts of the world and we learned a great deal about what we might expect to experience in mission ministry and in our own personal reactions.

I'll never forget our first gathering in Seminary Hall. Dr. Gottfried Oosterwahl had each of us come to the front and tell the rest of the group who we were, where we were going, and what we "thought" we were going to do once we got there. He was right on the money on that one!

The summer weeks at Andrews went by quickly and we had a few weeks to go back to the West Coast and visit family before leaving. This was certainly exciting for everyone concerned. My family was shocked and a little (or a lot) concerned for our decision. Ingrid's family, all Seventh-day Adventists, were reminded a bit of what it was like to leave Germany and travel to the United States. This was going to be a great adventure.

We flew out of San Francisco in August of 1979 and had a stop for several days in Hawaii. We had never been there before, so this was fantastic. The kids loved it and so did we. The next stop was Tokyo, where some of our new friends from Missions Institute were going to be working. We still have contact with so many of these dear people. We spent a night or two in Tokyo and we experienced our first meal eaten with chopsticks. The entrée was noodle soup. How in the world do you eat noodle soup with chopsticks? Well, if you're hungry you figure it out pretty quickly, but it can be a little messy.

Leaving Tokyo we now stopped for a day or two in Taipei, Taiwan where we were invited to dinner with Larry and Carol Colburn. This was a real treat as they were so gracious and encouraging. We stayed in mission housing at the Adventist Hospital. I recall breakfast in the apartment there. They had canned milk and granola along with a variety of fruit in the room. As the boys poured their milk on the cereal they couldn't help but notice that it seemed to be alive. Actually it was. They somehow didn't want to eat it, but I was brave (or dumb) and said that we were now in the mission field and I ate all of it. Yeah, it's been bugging me ever since!

Finally the day came around and we arrived in Hong Kong. It was a hot and muggy August day, but we were so excited to see our new home. Ward Hutton picked us up in the Hong Kong Adventist Hospital van and, of course, I started to get in the front seat and he just smiled and asked if I wanted to drive. I wasn't used to the steering wheel being on the right side of the car!

By the way, I should add that flying into Hong Kong's Kai Tak Airport in those days was an adventure all on its own! You would fly in over the city and the plane would bank sharply and had to almost fly between the buildings on the final approach. You could easily look into the flats and see what was happening. I loved that landing. Now they have built a new airport out on Lantau Island and it's not the same.

So, we arrived at the hospital, which was on Hong Kong Island while the airport was on the mainland in Kowloon. We were shown to our flat on the 6th floor and it had most of the furnishings that we would need. Our belongings had been so few and so light that they sent them by air rather than by ship and they arrived ahead of us and had been placed in the ground floor storage room. That turned out to be a problem because there had been a typhoon before we arrived and the room flooded. I lost a great many books in that mishap. They were insured, but many were not replaceable. We just chalked it up to mission experience.

I can't really put into words the feelings that we experienced in a move like this. The mission family was awesome in welcoming new workers and helping them to adjust. We were taken to the market to buy some fresh fruits and vegetables and taught a bit about how not to get ripped off in the process. We were also invited to a different home each night for the first week so that we could get acquainted and so that we wouldn't have to worry about fixing food. We were all very excited and began to build friendships that continue today.

The hardest thing we had ever done came just two days later when Ward took us back to the airport so that we could send our oldest son, Danny, to Singapore to attend Far Eastern Academy. That was 2,000 miles away and was a huge step for us all. He was a sophomore and was already a very big guy over six feet tall, but he was still our little boy. Neither Ingrid nor I could say a word all the way home in the van. Every time we tried we just got choked up and couldn't speak.

The Hong Kong years were absolutely marvelous for all of us. Our second son, Steve, went on to Far Eastern Academy the following year and our daughter, Julie started first grade shortly after we arrived. For the next six years she took the lift (elevator) from the 6th floor to the 12th floor each school day. Their play area, and our hospital cookout area, was on the roof.

The hospital chapel, where church services were held, was on the 6th floor of the hospital, which was directly across the drive from our block of flats. Many times, while pastoring in Coos Bay I had told this story: "We began ministry in eastern Iowa and then moved to central Iowa with three churches. Next we moved to western Iowa with two churches. Now we are on the Oregon coast with one church. I don't know where we will go next, but God can't move us any further west and He can't give us any fewer churches." Well, now He had moved us so much further west that we were in the Far East and we didn't have a church. We had a chapel. I think I heard God whisper in my ear, "Do you want to play again?" I didn't!

The Hong Kong years were crammed with opportunity. I soon found that it was easy, almost inevitable; to meet people who could make things happen. Hong Kong Adventist Hospital was designed to be the care center for Hong Kong's leaders and expatriates as well as for those who had contributed to the Adventist mission through the years. Whenever the President of the United States was in the vicinity our hospital was where he would have been taken. We had a state of the art cardiac center and simply offered the best care. What we didn't have, I realized, was a Health Education Department. I saw a great opportunity in that.

Let me back up just a bit. When we moved to Hong Kong I weighed in at over two hundred pounds. The running craze was just getting started there and several of the doctors and other missionaries were really into it. I had run track and cross country in high school and done quite well so I began to venture out with some of them. On my first run I couldn't go more than a quarter mile without stopping, but I kept at it and got great encouragement from many, especially Dr. Dale Morrison, head of the cardiology team. I figured he was a good one to run with!

Dale and the physical therapist, Arne Torkelsen, got together and started a running clinic based at the hospital that was modeled after the Honolulu Marathon Clinic and it was a success from the beginning. That began in the summer of 1980 and in March of 1981 a large group, including me, ran and completed our first marathons at the inaugural Coast of China Marathon. I was hooked!

That running clinic, which eventually swelled to over a thousand participants, drew people from all walks of life, including many influential Hong Kong businessmen and women. I could see that we needed to do more with health programming.

By the summer of 1982 we were able to take our first furlough and we came back to the U.S. for three months. We visited family and just reconnected with home. During that summer I ran the San Francisco Marathon and recorded my best time of 2 hours and 53 minutes. That's not world-class time, but it was respectable and put me in touch with other serious runners. During that summer I began to learn about ultra marathons. An ultra marathon is any run longer than a marathon. I had already participated in a couple of those in Hong Kong. Every year a small group of runners ran a race from the southernmost Police Station in Stanley, to the northernmost Police Station in Sha Tau Kok. It was always started and finished at those locations to "honor" the police for not allowing us to officially have the race! Now, on furlough, I began to think about the possibilities of ultra marathons.

Back in Hong Kong, I really felt the need to get an official Health Education Department going. I went to the Hospital Administrator, Laurie Dunfield, who is an absolutely delightful friend, and asked him for permission to initiate such a department. His first response was kind, but to the point, indicating that the hospital had no funding for that at this time. My next question was, "If I raise the money can we start one?" He thought that could be done. Then I asked him, "If I raise the money can I direct how it is spent?" He wisely counseled me to just raise the money first and we'd talk about the rest later.

I went for a run a few days later and came back to tell Ingrid that I'd had a brainstorm. She sat down. She always sits down after my brainstorms because they usually take some time to get used to. I told her that it was possible to raise money for the hospital's new Health Education Department (which didn't exist yet) by running for 24 hours and getting sponsors. I was excited about, and committed to, the project. She just thought I should be committed period, but she was used to that.

The preparations began in earnest. I began to talk to some of my running buddies, who often were also people who knew people who knew how to get things done. I also had one key church member in the person of Chan Shun, founder of the Crocodile Garment Factory. He and his son, Tom Chan, were interested in sponsoring the event and lended their contacts to the cause. They also donated clothing and made a generous financial contribution. I was able to get a number of influential corporate sponsors and the event was on.

Another running friend, David Griffiths, was the administrator at the Jubilee Sports Center in Kowloon. This was an absolute state of the art fitness complex complete with a running track. This was where Hong Kong's Olympic athletes trained. It also helped that a very dear friend,

Alan Wright, was the architect who had designed the complex. Alan was also part of our Running Clinic and had participated in several of our other health programs. This whole facility was made available to me for the actual run at no cost.

It did take a lot of planning work to put it all together, but there was excitement for the event among the hospital staff. This was clearly part fund-raising and part publicity and both were good for everyone involved. The newspapers were getting interested. One of the radio stations was going to give hourly reports on my progress and I had a large team of supporters from the hospital and from the running community. This would be a solo event, but the Jubilee Sports Center had requirements. I had to have a physician on hand that had the authority to end the event if he felt my health was in jeopardy. That was surely no problem, and Dr. Morrison was willing to be present. In fact I had quite a team of people who would spend the entire 24-hour period supporting me. I was excited.

I began the event at 8 pm on a Saturday night. It was a cool, but pleasant evening. The lights were on and the run began. A number of supporters would run with me for a few miles and then trade off. Every lap was counted and timed for accurate record keeping as this would also go into the Hong Kong Athletic Association Record Books. Obviously this was new territory for me and I was learning as I went. I had lined up the foods that I thought would replace my energy well. I had candy bars, energy drinks, fruit, and I don't even remember what all else. All I know is that nothing I brought worked.

I covered the first marathon distance in about three and a half hours, which was probably too fast, but I felt great. I hit the fifty-mile mark in about eight hours and then the weather turned bad. In fact it was very, very bad. The first seasonal monsoon hit and it started to pour with heavy winds. I had been reversing direction on the track every 20 laps, but now had to stick with the clockwise direction to give me some protection from the headwinds. I was soaked and I was cold. Every time Ingrid came out to run a lap with me I took her sweatshirt and was eventually wearing four at a time and still cold. I began to retreat into the hoods and they tell me I resembled a turtle and I had stopped conversing.

At 75 miles I was in trouble. I went in to the locker room and lay down on a table with some dry clothes. I was shaking uncontrollably from hypothermia in spite of being covered with several layers of blankets. I also had another problem in the form of stress fractures in both feet due to the rubberized asphalt surface of the track. That surface does not allow a runner to shuffle at all and the constant planting of my feet had done some damage. Dr. Morrison determined that I had to quit. This was devastating news to me and I begged him to allow me to continue. That's when an unusual thing happened.

John Wakefield was a crusty old sailor and a dear friend from the running community. His language and stories were often quite colorful, but he was much loved by all including our church connected running family. He barked out orders for them to take off the blankets and strip me down to my underwear. Next, he did the same and he lay down on the table and wrapped me in his arms. I asked him what in the world he was doing, but he simply told me to "Shut up and lay still." Within a few minutes time I stopped shaking and was warm from his body heat. I have often told that story since and used Ecclesiastes 4:9-12 to follow it up.

> **9** Two are better than one, because they have a good return for their work:
> **10** If one falls down, his friend can help him up. But pity the man who falls and has no one to help him up!
> **11** Also, if two lie down together, they will keep warm. But how can one keep warm alone?
> **12** Though one may be overpowered, two can defend themselves. A cord of three strands is not quickly broken.

Dr. Morrison gave permission for me to try a few laps. The wind and rain had let up quite a bit and I started out slow, but steady, and managed to cover another 28 miles for a total of 103 miles, which met my goal of 100 miles. The good news was that we got all of the sponsorship money, raised an awareness of the new programs to be offered at the hospital and were able to establish an official Health Education Department, of which I became the Director along with my pastoral/chaplaincy duties.

The first thing I did with the funding was to send myself to California to learn everything I could about various health education programs currently offered. I spent a great deal of time at Loma Linda University talking to everyone that I could and making a reading list. I also went to St. Helena Hospital and to Weimar Institute. I then went to several bookstores and bought every book that had been recommended and was now ready to return to Hong Kong.

We had already put out a schedule of programs that included multiple Stop Smoking Programs, each one followed by a six-week Stress Management Program, First-Aid classes, Pre-Natal classes, Cooking Schools, and we also offered classes on basic Bible teachings. Some of these courses, such as the First-Aid and Pre-Natal were already being offered and taught by Barbara Morrison who worked with me in the Health Education Department. These were wonderful and very fulfilling times!

I ended up repeating that fund raising run the next two years, but in a new location. Believe it or not I was able to obtain the full use of the Hong Kong Government Stadium (where the Billy Graham Crusade was held) for $100 HK (about $12 US) and it had a cinder track, which allowed me to shuffle my feet as fatigue set in. I accomplished 105 miles and 114 miles in the next efforts.

The night before I was to return to Hong Kong I was visiting my parents in Sequim, Washington. The phone rang and it was the President of the Far Eastern Division in Singapore, Winston Clark, calling to inform me of an "opportunity." It seems that the Division evangelist had become ill and was scheduled for a series of meetings in Dumaguete, on the southern tip of Negros Island in the Philippines. He informed me that I was needed to take those meetings, which would begin in just one week. I explained to him that I had been gone for a month and was just getting back and that I had new programs scheduled for just over a month away and needed to put together my presentations.

He said, "I don't think you understand. The evangelist is sick. No one from here can go and we need you to do this." My last attempt at protest was, "But I've been gone from my wife for a month already." His response was, "I just talked to her on the phone and she said it was OK!" I wasn't sure what all to read into that, but it was obvious I was going to the Philippines.

Elder Clark then gave me the phone number of the Mission President in the Philippines, Oscar Alalor, and told me that he was waiting for my call. He said that I needed to call him in the next hour with my twenty-six sermon titles. Now, I had done some evangelism before, but I didn't just have twenty-six sermons ready. He "comforted" me with the fact that it wasn't necessary to have the sermons ready. I just needed the titles. My parents just watched in amazement at what was going on as I plotted out a series of topics, chose titles, and called halfway around the world.

I returned to Hong Kong, unpacked, repacked, and just a few days later was on my way to Dumaguete. Flying into this smallish city is an adventure in itself. There is only one runway and, in fact, there is only one flight per day. Thirty minutes before arrival time the locals removed the water buffalo from the runway and they also remove what the water buffalo leave behind! The runway extends right out to the beach so you can't see land until just as you touch down, which makes for an interesting sensation.

The Mission President, Oscar Alalor, met me at the airport and he asked if I would first like to see where the meetings were going to be held. Of course I was ready for almost anything at this point. We drove in his Jeep to the "downtown" area and he showed me a vacant lot. I was a bit taken back by this as I had imagined the meetings in a church or some kind of hall, but I remarked that open-air meetings would be interesting. "Oh no," he informed me, "we will have a church building here. We start building it tomorrow." This was Thursday afternoon and the meetings were to begin on Sunday evening. The next morning I was up early to witness this challenge.

Sure enough, early Friday morning, several trucks loaded with building materials arrived as well as a truckload of workers. The building was simple with sidewalls that only went halfway up. This was partly for ventilation in the humid evenings and partly so that the people outside the building (nearly as many as inside) would be able to hear as well. By Friday evening the walls were up, the corrugated metal roof was on, the platform was in place and they were ready to install lighting.

On Sabbath I was taken to preach in one of the outlying villages and had a wonderful day of fellowship along with a marvelous fellowship meal. On Sunday, when I was brought back to the meeting place I was truly amazed. Not only was everything finished and ready, but also the stage had a backdrop that had a colored cellophane artistic depiction of the first night's topic. On each of the twenty-six nights there was a different artistic work related to that night's subject. That was why they needed those titles in advance.

One other experience happened here that had a major impact on this young preacher's spiritual journey. These meetings served as a field school of evangelism for more than twenty area pastors. Each day I would go with one of them to visit homes in the nearby barrios (villages). I enjoyed this experience immensely once I got used to Philippine time, which was not quite as punctual as American time. Most days I traveled with the pastor on the back of his motorcycle, which was certainly not the same size as my transportation this summer. As we arrived in each barrio we would visit each of the homes. This was a fascinating experience. The homes were all raised up off the ground and they had no door. You had to climb up a ladder or a steep set of stairs and simply call out, "Knocking, knocking!" I always made them let me do that part. It was like a doorbell with an American accent!

Toward the end of the meetings I was having one such day of visitation and announced myself at another home. The lady of the house came to the door and invited us in. During the four weeks of meetings we never had one home that did not invite us in to visit. I thought often how unlikely that would be back in America. These simple homes were always very clean and neat. This beautiful lady invited us into the back room (there were only two) where her husband was sick in bed. She told us that he had been unable to leave the bed for more than six months. He had some kind of palsy and was unable to walk. We visited for a short time and talked about her family, my family, and the meetings that were being held. As we prepared to leave I asked to pray and they, as each family did, readily agreed.

Taking the man by the hand I began my prayer with the pastor, the wife, and two teenage daughters gathered around the bed. My prayer was not a prayer for healing, but rather one for a blessing on this family. I mentioned the meetings, the family, and then asked a blessing on the father. As the prayer began to focus on him I felt his grip strengthen and sensed that he was drawing strength from my prayer. I also felt impressed to focus my prayer now for his physical healing. I remember praying that in the Bible there were men with similar illnesses that had been healed and we acknowledged that God had the power to heal my brother as well. Immediately a strange sensation flowed through me that would have to describe as a tingling, almost electrical feeling. I felt power flow into his hands and was aware that he was no longer trembling, but I was!

Finishing the prayer and looking down at my friend. I said, "You're better aren't you?" He looked back, and with a twinkle in his eye he said, "No, I'm not better. I'm healed." With that he proceeded to get up and got out of the bed and began to walk around the room. He lifted his legs high and began to almost jog in place. I looked at his wife and saw that she was weeping. His daughters, too, were crying and so was the pastor. Not wanting to be left out, I cried as well. I had never experienced anything like this in my life. My nature is to be quite skeptical. My middle name is Thomas and Ingrid says I was well named.

This experience has changed my whole outlook on prayer for healing. I am now, obviously, convinced that God has the ability and power to heal any kind of disease. I am also fully aware that most diseases, even if seriously prayed for, are not healed. We can take that even a step further when we recognize that every person that Jesus healed later died. It doesn't even suggest that they lived longer than average. The miracle of healing is not really about the healing. Rather, it is about a God who has the power to regenerate life. ***James, chapter 5, teaches me that the prayer of faith, accompanied by anointing, is about surrender more than about healing.*** If we surrender, God will forgive and He will raise us up, if not miraculously now, then miraculously at the second coming. I believe this experience in the Philippines was at least as much for my spiritual healing as for my friend's physical healing.

The following Sunday I was to fly back to Hong Kong in the afternoon. That morning I connected with the same pastor who had experienced this miracle with me and asked him if he would take me back to the same home and he was happy to do so. I wanted to see if the miracle was real. Had it lasted? Oh me of little faith!

We rode on his motorcycle directly to the same home. I hopped off the back and climbed the ladder and called out my greeting. This time it was not the lady who came to the door, but rather it was my brother. He was so delighted to see me and said that he had a funny story to tell me. I love funny stories and so he shared the following experience.

"The day after you left I went out into the central gathering area." (This is a circular space with cooking areas on the perimeter and serves as the "living room" of the barrio.) "This was the first time I had been outside of the house in over six months. When everyone else in the barrio saw me they got up and went to their homes and stayed there all day because they thought I had died and they were seeing my ghost." He was having a hard time containing his delight as he shared this story. As for me, I was filled with a new faith in a God of miracles!

With that conclusion we returned to Dumaguete and I boarded my plane back to Hong Kong. Once there it was necessary to throw myself into the preparation for a wide variety of programs and the development and promotion of the Health Education Department of the Hong Kong Adventist Hospital.

When we conducted the first Hong Kong Health Fair we were able to obtain donated advertising from the third largest advertising company in the world and PR from a leading Public Relations firm. The Hong Kong Government Health Department also got involved. We were often invited to participate in radio talk shows and I even conducted an "on air" stop smoking program in which the host went through the steps and stopped smoking herself. These were fantastically fun years where enlisting help from 'movers and shakers' was not difficult and a great deal of advancement in the community outreach of the hospital was accomplished. This was not because of my abilities. It was simply my privilege to be in the right place at the right time with the right people. The Hong Kong years of 1979–1985 were marvelous years for all of our family and full of rich and wonderful memories and friends that we cherish to this day.

It was also during this time that I began to really grow in my own spiritual journey and understanding of and focus on faith in Christ alone as the heart and soul of the work I was called to do. This process came a bit painfully at times.

We were so privileged to have the Chans as one of our church families in the Hong Kong Adventist Hospital Church. Chan Shun was the founder and head of the Crocodile Garment Company as I mentioned before. His story is a miracle in itself, as he became one of the denomination's most prolific philanthropists. I believe that most, if not all, of our colleges and universities have buildings named after him due to his generous donations. More than that, he, and his son Tom like him, were and are just genuinely lovely Christian men and all of the family echoes that character. Dr. Chan's daughter, Pearl, was the organist for our church and a group in the church family asked me to speak to her about her red fingernail polish. I am shaking my head in remorse while I write this right now when I tell you that I somehow felt it was my pastoral duty to carry out their wishes. I did indeed share with her how disturbing that was to some of the church family and I will never forget the look of pain upon her face. She was not argumentative. She was not resistant, but she was deeply hurt and now she has passed away and I can't ask her forgiveness. At that moment I knew that God had not called me to determine the color of fingernails, or the standards of my parishioners. He had called me to preach the gospel of our Lord Jesus Christ and allow Him to direct the lives of His own children. May God forgive me for the times I have broken the "Hippocratic Oath" (to first do no harm) of the Great Physician.

In May of 1985 we left Hong Kong. Our sons were now at Pacific Union College and we felt we needed to come back to the U.S. and continue ministry there. Our daughter was heartbroken. This was the only home she really knew and she wanted remain in Hong Kong and go on to Far Eastern Academy in Singapore like her brothers, but it was not to be. Instead we moved from the British Colony of Hong Kong, with its eight million inhabitants to the bustling metropolis of Bozeman, Montana! If you want an illustration of culture shock, it is not moving from Coos Bay, Oregon to Hong Kong, but rather moving from Hong Kong to Bozeman, Montana!

The truth is that it was not all that easy to assimilate back into the stream of pastoral opportunities back home. Many of the contacts I had when we left Oregon were no longer in those same positions and we couldn't exactly pick and choose. That is not at all to say that Bozeman was not a wonderful experience for us. It was, however, a challenging transition.

Our daughter, Julie, suffered the most. Consider a twelve year old girl who has only known the school commute of taking the elevator from the sixth floor to the twelfth floor and there she mixes with students from many different nationalities as well as American friends who have traveled the world. Now she transitions to a three-mile commute to a sprawling campus with classmates who haven't shared much, if any, of her experiences. Suffice it to say that Julie really struggled to adjust. She did make many new great friends, but had great difficulty in identifying with their "norms."

I also found the adjustment challenging. I think we all did. In Hong Kong I had been involved in major events and had been fairly well known in the greater community at large. I had enjoyed the privilege of serving as a Committee Chairman with the American Chamber of Commerce. Now I was totally unknown in a small western town. I'm sure that was good for me. I'll never forget a conversation with one local resident. He had asked me if we were enjoying Bozeman and I said that we thought it was a great little town. He took some exception to the adjective "little" and I tried to explain it to him like this; "Where we just moved from there were single apartment complexes with more than three times the population of this town. Each complex has it's own school, hospital, and shopping area. Many such complexes make up just one area of a single area of the city." He just looked at me, shook his head, and walked away.

In Bozeman I was the pastor of the Bozeman City Church and along with that was the Director of the Montana Conference Church Ministries Department. That meant that one week I would preach in Bozeman and on alternate weeks would take appointments in one of the conference churches. I did enjoy all of this, but found it hard to do real justice to either position.

I think it would be well to end this chapter with a tribute to Ingrid and to other pastoral spouses. Every time we moved Ingrid had to find new employment. I had a job and a "calling." She had to scramble and take what she could find. She has loved all of our years of ministry, but that doesn't mean it has been easy or always fun. In Hong Kong she began working for the church as secretary to the Hospital President, Laurie Dunfield. In Bozeman she was fortunate to have the opportunity to become the secretary to Herman Bauman, the Conference President. Later on there would be breaks in her denominational employment, but to date she has accumulated more than twenty-three years of service and she is currently the Administrative Secretary to John Rasmussen, Treasurer of the Northern California Conference. She has been in that position for the past ten years and I have promised her that we will not move until she retires. Those of us in ministry owe a great deal of love and honor to our faithful, sacrificing spouses!

I did turn 40 in Bozeman and that ends the fourth decade of my journey. I get great joy in telling our boys that they are now older than I was when we were in Bozeman. As that reality hits them, they get a dazed look in their eyes. I have asked each of them, "You thought I was old then didn't you?" The look tells me that I was right.

Chapter the Ninth

The Fifth Week

WRAY, COLORADO

I left Ogallala fairly early Sunday morning, beginning this fifth week of my journey. My first destination was part project and part pure fun. I was headed to Wray, Colorado. Ingrid and I had been through here back in 1990 and I wanted to stop again as part of the trip. This is the only town in the U.S. that bears my surname. The interesting thing is that there are no Wrays in the phone book or in the cemetery. A cattleman by the name of Thomas Wray used to drive cattle through here and took a liking to the area and was able to convince enough others of its possibilities that a town was established. A few years later good old Tom moved on and evidently didn't leave any family behind. We enjoyed seeing such names as the Wray Bank, Wray Oil Company, and, of course, the Wray Liquor Store. I also have a shoulder patch from the Wray Police Department on my office desk. We also were delighted to find the Wray Seventh-day Adventist Church during that visit and I was anxious to find out how it was doing.

The ride from Ogallala to Wray was beautiful with gorgeous sunshine making the golden fields of wheat look like a vast store of treasure. The first few miles were still on I-80, but then I headed south on Hwy 385 in Colorado. I stopped a couple of times just to take in the beauty of it all. By 9:00 am it was already in the 80's and the landscape was changing from flat to rolling hills and the beauty of the day was really shining through. Entering the town itself I was quite disappointed to see many of the stores on the main street boarded up. The whole town looked like it was getting near to closing time. I didn't spend much time in town and headed westward out of the city limits toward where I remembered the church was located. What a great disappointment it was to find that although there was still a highway sign giving directions to the church, the building itself was boarded up and lifeless. I took a few pictures and sadly headed west.

Riding on the state highways is so much more enjoyable than the interstates. US 385 coming into Wray was fabulous and now US 34 heading west was just as wonderful. I had ridden just 100 miles in the early part of the day and now Brighton was 150 miles away. It was necessary to hook up with I-76 for the last part of the ride. I will say, however, that the interstates in most of the Midwest are not nearly as bad as in the big cities.

BRIGHTON, COLORADO

I had hoped to meet with Rex Bell, Sr. Pastor of the Brighton, CO SDA Church, but he was not available on this Sunday morning. I had a delightful visit instead with Todd Belleau and his son, Caleb. Todd is the School Board Chairman and the school is the real focal point of the ministry and outreach of the church here.

Typical of most SDA churches, Brighton has a membership of 500 and about half that number in average attendance. The school is pre-K through 10 and has about 130 students currently. It has been higher in the past as is the case with most schools. The Brighton church is the only sponsoring church and it requires a major portion of their finances. ***Rex Bell holds two garage sales every month and raises $800-1200 each sale to support worthy students. That's about $24,000 a year, but their worthy student cost is closer to $80,000 plus a subsidy of another $100,000. That's commitment to education. They do have many non-SDA students and this has been a rich source of baptisms for students and parents. These families are also the biggest promoters of the school.***

Todd did share with me that enrollment used to be higher and it is getting to be a greater and greater challenge to keep the funding going. This is sad because they have found that parents who get involved with the school early on tend to stay active in the church. ***I have found that all around the country it is becoming increasingly difficult to maintain our Adventist schools. Costs are going up and commitment is going down. This is going to present some unique challenges to the Brighton Church family as well as everywhere else.***

This is a particularly beautiful church facility and sits in a great location. ***I have found that most of our churches are kept in good condition and are attractive. Obviously, this is not enough. People will not swarm to our congregations just because they are well located and beautiful. Many of the storefront congregations and home churches are growing much faster because of relationships and having real needs met.*** In Brighton the school has been successful in doing that in the past. The question now is whether or not that is still the same perceived need in the minds of the church and the community.

BERTHOUD, COLORADO – GRACE PLACE

Just 40 miles north of Brighton is the fairly small community of Berthoud. This is where I would spend Sunday evening with friends I hadn't seen in a long time. Clay and Selene Peck live in Berthoud where Clay is the lead pastor at Grace Place, which also has a campus in Loveland, a few more miles north. This is an amazing ministry and that is a classic understatement.

They were involved in a church outing that Sunday afternoon and I got into the area before they returned home. Thankfully I found a Starbucks just down the road and ducked in out of the rain to do some computer catching up. I also had the privilege of connecting with more "old" friends who lived nearby. Roger and Debbie Peterson were members back in the early Iowa days and I had stayed with Roger's sister, Darla, the previous Friday night. What a blessing it was to connect again, if only for an hour or so. Family and friends are so precious and it is wonderful to realize again that you can go for years without any contact and still pick up where you left off. Thanks, friends, for taking the time to drive on down and visit!

I first got acquainted with Clay and Selene Peck when I was the Ministerial Director in the Potomac Conference and Clay was the pastor in Davenport, Iowa where I first started ministry. We had talked on the phone a few times and were interested in having Clay come to pastor at the Courthouse Road Church just outside of Richmond, Virginia. During that process Ingrid and I happened to be driving across the country to visit family and we stopped overnight not far from Davenport. On Friday morning I called the Peck's home about 7:00, assuming that with small children they would be up. Selene answered and I introduced myself and told her that one of the things I like to do before extending an official invitation to pastor a church is to stop by on a Friday morning to see if the family is ready for Sabbath.

I remember that there was just this dead silence on the phone so I quickly added that I was just kidding. We were just passing through and hoped that they would be up and wondered if we could take them to breakfast and get a little better acquainted. I'm not sure if Selene has ever forgiven me, but she didn't poison my food on this trip.

I was immediately impressed by this couple back then and I continue to admire and respect their ministry today. Grace Place began as a church plant back in the mid 90's. Let me just share the info directly from the Grace Place website to briefly tell the story.

For years Pastor Clay Peck dreamed of planting a new, gospel-centered, creative and contemporary congregation, which would especially reach out to people who were disconnected from God or from church. In August of 1995 he wrote a document on his computer entitled, "What If?" where he outlined steps to take in starting a new congregation if the opportunity ever presented itself. Clay, having grown up in Colorado, even wrote down a dream location – "a bedroom community north of Denver, Colorado." Clay and his wife, Selene, decided to put it before the Lord in prayer.

In December of that year a small group of Christian friends met together in Fort Collins, Colorado to discuss the possibility of starting a new church that would be fresh, relevant and outreach-oriented. Through what now seems like a series of miracles, they came across Clay's name and asked him to come do a weekend presentation. Clay talked about the importance of keeping the gospel of grace the main thing. Relationships were developed that led to a decision to team up together to launch a new congregation.

Clay and his family moved to Colorado in June of 1996. Throughout that summer the expanding core group met in mountain parks for informal worship, fellowship, and vision casting. We studied biblical principles for how a healthy church should be planted and participated in the first membership class. Grace Place began officially with our first public worship service the second weekend of September 1996 at the Berthoud High School.

From the start, Grace Place was a regional congregation with participants coming from cities surrounding Berthoud. For the first four years the church met in rented facilities. Due to schedule conflicts we bounced around to different locations including the Metrolux Theaters in Loveland, Longmont High School, a couple different churches in Longmont (where we shared the facility), and Turner Middle School in Berthoud.

The congregation numbered just over 200 when we remodeled and moved into our own building at 250 Mountain Ave. Since then we have grown to more than 1000 with multiple weekend services. Grace Place has become a seven-day-a-week ministry, building bridges to the community through creative endeavors such as The Lighthouse Café and Five Stones Student Center. In the fall of 2007 Grace Place became a multi-site church, worshipping in both Berthoud and Loveland. Stay tuned—the best is yet to come!

Clay took me on a tour of the Berthoud campus, which is comprised of several buildings spread throughout the community. I was particularly impressed with the youth building, "Five Stones", and even more impressed when I stepped inside. Here I found a snack bar, a caged basketball court, multiple game tables and computer stations and a variety of other things to interest youth.

At this particular time the youth themselves were involved in "Sundae Night Fights." No, I didn't misspell "Sundae." They were out in the back lot throwing ice cream, chocolate sauce, and whipping cream at each other. Now there's a unique ministry! They were open enough to invite me to join them, but somehow I resisted the temptation. I will say, however, they were having a great time and they were involved. Hey, you can burn off the calories while you eat them! There is another separate building for the junior age youth as well.

The worship center is not as large as I was expecting, but they have multiple services each Sunday and throughout the week. They also have the Grace Place Café, which serves regular fare through the week. I had the best breakfast burrito I've ever had there on Monday morning.

You can check out their website at www.graceplace.org, and I encourage you to do just that. This ministry did start out as a Seventh-day Adventist church plant. They are no longer a Seventh-day Adventist congregation. That is a long story that Clay shared openly with me. While I personally regret having lost Clay and Selene from our denominational team I praise God for the ministry God has enabled them to establish and for the lives that Grace Place is touching. ***I am not defending or judging here. I am only observing that I saw methods and intent visible at Grace Place that were effective, Christ centered, and joyful. We can learn a lot by observing with open hearts and minds and I learned a ton in Berthoud. I also cherished the opportunity to renew a dear friendship.***

GREAT OPEN SPACES OF COLORADO AND WYOMING

After that great breakfast burrito I was anxious to get on the road and greatly looking forward to the day's ride. Today there would be no church interviews. Instead there would be many miles of gorgeous riding through northern Colorado and Wyoming as I headed toward Montana. The plains were behind me, and the mountains, and mostly state highways, were before me. This was going to be fun!

I did start out with interstates, beginning on I-25 north out of Colorado and heading west on I-80 as far as Rawlins. However, in this part of the country even the interstates are not a burden and the scenery is still mighty fantastic! I stopped for a short visit to the huge statue of Lincoln that you can't miss near Laramie. This marks the highest elevation on I-80 at something over 8,000 feet.

One of the fun parts of a trip like this is stopping at scenic areas. It seems there are always a few who want to look over the bike and find out where you're from and where you're going. On this trip I single handedly caused a major amount of drool in many men. The thought of having six weeks to cover 12,000 miles on a motorcycle and still be on salary seemed to be enough to leave them dazed until bored wives hauled them back to the reality of the kids who were more than ready to go somewhere fun!

In Rawlins I turned north on Hwy 287 and found that the wind, which had already been significant, now got severe. My Valkyrie has a 5.5 gallon tank with another gallon in a reserve. I normally average around 35 miles per gallon on my bike. I could do better if I slowed down to 65, but rolling along at 75 - 80 just seems to work a lot better and is still will within the acceptable range of the highway patrol when the limit is usually at least 70 anyway. However, on this stretch I got well under 20 mpg and by the time I stopped for the night in Dubois I felt like I'd been in a fight. It was that night that I remembered something I had tucked away before I left home so many weeks before.

My Head Elder, Ron Wisbey, had given me an envelope that was simply addressed; "Somewhere In America." He had told me that it could be opened anywhere and I had packed it in one of the saddlebags. I had thought about it a few times, but was saving it for some point when I needed a lift in spirits. I am surprised that I didn't open it the night after my ride through the horrendous thunderstorm, but I guess I was so thankful that night to be with dear friends in Lincoln, Nebraska and had a chance to rest and enjoy the Sabbath and even get some laundry done that I just didn't think of it then. But this night I felt a strong mix of emotions. I was five and a half weeks into the trip, was still a long way from home and was beginning to really feel anxious to get there. Still, I knew that there were appointments to keep and many visits that I was looking forward to. I had ridden nearly 9,000 miles thus far, so the novelty had worn off and yet I didn't really want the adventure to end. I don't know if you can understand that apparent contradiction or not, to be anxious to be home and yet not ready to give up the journey.

So it was on that Monday night in Dubois, Wyoming as I sat in a "so-so" motel room, thankful to be there just before the rains came hard and contemplating what I had experienced, but feeling very alone, that I opened the envelope "Somewhere in America". In that letter I found a great message of affirmation for what I was doing. I was assured that I was missed by the home church even though they were in the very capable hands of my associates, John Grys and Sherilyn O'Ffill. The letter expressed the belief that my sabbatical project was worthwhile and would be a blessing to the church at large and it reminded me that I was being prayed for daily by the entire church family for safety and success. That letter, that night, made a huge difference in my heart.

Throughout my journey my sweet and patient wife had prepared cards for me to open every few days with reminders of her love and prayers. This project was as much of a sacrifice for her as it was an adventure for me. Every night I anxiously looked forward to the opportunity to Skype with her. Being able to see her face and to pray with her "in person" kept me going. I'm not sure how I'll ever pay her back, but I acknowledge that I owe her big time!

YELLOWSTONE PARK & BOZEMAN, MONTANA

Tuesday morning dawned clear and cold and the report was that there was a lot of road construction between Dubois and Yellowstone so I left at about 6:45 in hopes of getting through before work started. My hopes were dashed! It would take me more than three hours to cover the next 85 miles! The one-way traffic was operating 24 hours a day and I was stopped for as much as a half hour in one area. I was feeling some pressure to get through because I was having new tires put on again just outside of Bozeman, Montana and I needed to be there in the early afternoon in order for them to have time to accomplish the job. Remember, in order to change my rear tires you have to take off the saddlebags and the six exhaust pipes. To accomplish the latter you have to wait a significant length of time for them to cool off. It takes about three hours to get it done. The delays were pleasant at times, however, in that I had some great conversations with workers and travelers alike and often the scenery at the stops was spectacular. Even though I was pressed for time I had to make several stops to take pictures along Jackson Lake, Lewis Lake, and for some amazing shots of the Grand Tetons.

Finally I made it through the construction area and entered into Yellowstone National Park. How glad I was that the year before when we went on a church campout in Yosemite and I was able to purchase that lifetime Senior pass to all of the national parks for the amazing sum of ten dollars! Yes, there are advantages to being a senior citizen!

Inside the park I was on the lookout for wildlife photo opportunities. I didn't see anything coming in from the south. I stopped at Old Faithful and was fortunate to see it spout off just a few minutes after I arrived. It felt good to stretch my legs on the walk from the parking lot to the geyser. Old Faithful isn't what it used to be. The pressure seems to be somewhat controlled and regulated and it didn't shoot nearly as high as I had seen it in years past, but it was still fun, especially to hear the "oohs and aahs" of the children present.

Quickly back in the saddle I rode out toward West Yellowstone. I had passed along here so many times when we lived in Bozeman and I never failed to see wildlife, especially buffalo. Today, however, I saw absolutely nothing. I suppose that the noise from my six exhaust pipes could have something to do with it, but I didn't have time to wait or to search so I just left the camera in the bag and kept on going.

I stopped for gas in West Yellowstone and then headed up north toward Gallatin Gateway. The road weaves in and out between Montana and Wyoming and the scenery is great the entire way. As I rode past Big Sky I noticed some amazing changes in the amount of development for both summer and winter resort opportunities. In some ways it was sad to see so much development, but that's progress, or so they say.

At last I made it to Powerplay Motorsports to drop the bike off for service and new tires. I had only put a little over 8,000 miles on this set of rubber, but I wouldn't have another chance and I don't like the prospects of having a blowout. I like the 'better safe than sorry' approach to long distance riding.

Our dear friend, Sylvia Grindley, picked me up at the bike shop. I would be staying with Jim and Sylvia that evening and while we waited for the bike to be serviced she took me all around the Bozeman area to show me the changes since we had lived there. We drove out past our old house near Hyalite Canyon, went past the Bozeman City Church where

I had pastored and on out to Mt. Ellis Academy and the new Montana Conference Office nearby. Bozeman is a very beautiful city and it was so much fun to see how much things had grown since we left twenty-two years before. We returned to pick up the bike and nearly $900 later I was riding again. Yes, tires are expensive and, as I mentioned earlier, there is significant labor involved to install them. I also had the regular service that includes oil and filter and other maintenance checks. Thankfully, that was the last service I would need on the trip.

Now we had a fantastic meal at the Grindley home and following that I had the opportunity to sit down with a great group representing leadership from both the City Church and the Academy Church. I met with the current Bozeman pastor, Jim Jenkins and his head elder, Linda Nystrom (yet another woman serving as head elder) and her husband Clair, Doug Meharry, head elder at the Mount Ellis Academy Church and Tom Glatz who pastored in Kalispell recently and is moving to Vancouver, B.C. to pastor. ***One thing in particular I thought was cool was related to the Bozeman City Church. They are located next to the high school and have had ongoing problems with graffiti and other worse things on their property. They started feeding lunch to the kids who cross through the church parking lot one day a week and the problems have stopped. They hand out literature about drugs and alcohol and have had some very positive results. I love that kind of creative approach that turns a problem into an opportunity. They could have built a bigger fence, but they chose to open a door instead and turn a problem into a blessing. I think Jesus smiled when He saw that.***

The City Church also participates with LOVE INC (Love In the Name of Christ), which works with a wide variety of churches to combat the need for food, clothing, shelter, and other areas for families in need of help. I think it is a great thing when somewhat smaller churches that cannot sustain a major outreach on their own can partner with other churches and other denominations to do a greater work. Sometimes it is as valuable to simply work with others as part of a team as it is to sustain a work in our name exclusively.

Mt. Ellis Academy is a very special place. It has a unique and gorgeous setting and opportunities for students that simply are not available at many of our schools. It also has an alumni program second to none. I would simply encourage you to Google Mt. Ellis Academy, and see some of the things that are happening there and how the Lord has blessed this school. ***They serve as a host site for Family Promise, which is an interdenominational ministry to minister to the homeless.***

The Kalispell Church reaches their community in a wide variety of ways. They sponsor 3ABN Radio and Life Talk Radio and have students selling the Megabook offerings in the summer. They hold Depression Classes for the community and offer Bible Study training for members. Kalispell is a beautiful place near Glacier National Park and Flathead Lake. If you don't mind cold winters it's a great place to live and the church is certainly active in the community.

Montana is not an easy place to grow churches. It is a small conference with a huge territory and many of the locals tend to be fairly well set in their ways and yet the work goes on. ***God's work is not about huge numbers all the time. His Kingdom is built one life at a time and each one is precious.*** There is a close family bond and hardiness in the members here and it was wonderful to be a part of it one more time.

GREAT FALLS & HELENA, MONTANA

Wednesday morning I was off early again. This time the destination was first to Helena for a breakfast appointment with Darrin and Loy Dixon. Darrin and his wife, Joan, were members of ours in Napa and we had built a strong friendship there. During this time, Joan was expecting and came down with a rare form of leukemia. We grew even closer as she worked through treatments and pregnancy. She did deliver a beautiful daughter, Alexandria, but sadly Joan died about six months later. Her memorial was held near Lincoln, Nebraska and we flew out to conduct the service. The following year I had the privilege of performing the wedding for Darrin and Loy, who had been Joan's roommate in medical school. Life takes some strange twists on the way to the Kingdom sometimes. The trick is to stay in His arms long enough to allow Him to complete the journey!

The ride from Bozeman to Helena is gorgeous, as is every ride through western Montana I think. The three of us met at an IHOP and spent a couple of lovely hours just catching up, sharing, praying, and simply being together. One of the greatest rewards of ministry is having so many with whom you have shared so much. Through baptisms, weddings, funerals, and life in general, bonds are built that will last into eternity.

The Dixons live in Great Falls, Montana and were in the midst of a pastoral change at a time when they and the church needed strong leadership. I am happy to report as of this writing that Pr. Greg Jones has more than met their needs and expectations. Darrin and Loy have such a passion for outreach and sharing the good news of the gospel as it is in Jesus and I'm looking forward to hearing good things come from this church.

Now riding from Helena west on Hwy 12 and over MacDonald Pass I encountered scenery that was nothing short of breathtaking. I wanted to stop at every curve in the road and just let the rugged beauty sink in. The elevation gets up to about 6300 feet and it seems like you can see forever. Once again I felt the sting of scheduling as I had to get to Coeur d' Alene, Idaho for an evening appointment and then as far west as I could get before fatigue took complete control. I would love to make this entire trip again, only next time with Ingrid and perhaps in a car, and have the time to stop whenever we wanted to stop. However, there was only so much time and I had mapped out a mission to be accomplished so my stops must be limited. On through Avon, on to I-90, and the bike kept heading west. The ride consists of 280 miles of continuous beauty, but it was already about 11:00 when I left Helena. The good news was that I would pick up an extra hour on the way.

COEUR D' ALENE, IDAHO

Actually, when I arrived in Coeur d' Alene I found there was a little time to kill so I found a trusty Starbucks and caught up on some much needed blog updating and phone calls related to the days to come. Scheduling was always on my mind and there were so many unknowns to deal with. Looking back on it all I am amazed and very thankful to God for His guidance and blessings on my way. I only missed one appointment heading east and one coming back, but the last one has an explanation that I hope you will understand. There will be more about that in chapter eleven. At the appointed hour I met with Phil Muthersbaugh, first in his office and then in his home with about a dozen of his church family. ***I must say that this group was absolutely "FUN" and alive with a passion for the gospel and connecting with His children. All I know is that I was loved, cared for, prayed over, and blessed. If I felt that in one evening, how would a visitor feel after attending for a few weeks? Well, they would feel loved, cared for, prayed over and blessed and I am guessing that they would want to come back and stay.***

The LifeSource Community Church makes no apologies for being unique. In fact it was their intention. Let me just share a couple of paragraphs from their website:

At LifeSource, you'll find people from all walks of life - younger, older, single, married, divorced, working, stay-at-home, retired, unemployed, to name a few. We're people just like you, all working together at growing closer to God, our Source of authentic and abundant life and loving others like Jesus modeled it. We're not perfect and we don't have all the answers, but we'd love for you to join us for Sabbath (Saturday) worship or any of our other exciting ministries and events.

We are people ***reaching out****... in the name of Jesus to friends, to family, to our community, and to those in need through meaningful relationships. We are people* ***reaching up****... to God as we learn to love and follow Jesus and pattern our lives after his. We are people* ***reaching forward****... because of Jesus' promise to return to this earth again very soon. We believe it is our "mission" to share this Good News with everyone in our community.*

Currently they meet in a rented facility, but they have tremendous access available in their agreement. It works, at least for now, very well. ***They are definitely a more contemporary styled church, but very solidly Seventh-day Adventist and another group that is just so warm and loving that it's hard not to want to stay.***

LifeSource launched in April of 2004 and has grown in their ministry offerings very quickly. As with all of the churches I have covered I would encourage you to find them on the internet and take a look for yourself at what they have going on. ***Here you will find an abundant list of ministries reaching the church body and the community both with the message of unconditional love.*** I wish I could have stayed for Sabbath worship, but that was not possible. Maybe I can do that in the future. Thanks, Phil, and church family for a wonderful evening.

As of this writing I understand that Phil has moved on and I do not know who his replacement will be. I am sure, however, that the real strength in LifeSource is in the leadership, passion, and compassion of the lay membership. It will be fun to see how this plays out in the next few years.

I had originally planned to stay overnight in Coeur d' Alene, but I opted to ride further west as I needed to be in Yakima, Washington fairly early the next morning and I didn't want to go through Spokane traffic in the morning rush hour. So, even though it was dark I left and rode for about an hour and a half before checking in to a motel for a little rest.

Thursday morning was cool, but crystal clear and I was heading into very familiar territory riding through eastern Washington as we had spent much time there in my childhood. I left the motel at 5:30 in the morning in order to cover the 200 miles and arrive by 9:00. Keep in mind that I have to stop more frequently for gas than if in a car and there are always the multiple photo opportunities and I don't want to have to pass them all!

I loved this part of the ride. The sky was clear. The morning was cool, but I had plenty of warm clothes while riding through the Palouse region. As a boy we used to go over to Coulee Dam, Wenatchee, Yakima, and Leavenworth every summer and I grew to love the dry climate and the rolling hills. Soon Mt. Adams and then Mt. Rainier came into view. These giants leaped out from the ground and into the sky and I think they are particularly beautiful from the east side. Finally I descended down gently curving roads into Yakima to find the Connections Church of Yakima and meet with the Lead Pastor, Shane Del Vecchio.

YAKIMA, WASHINGTON

Connections meets in the Vineyard Church right downtown. I pulled into a street parking spot and was taking off my leathers to make myself just a bit more presentable and comfortable and Shane came out of the church. His office is in the basement, but he said he heard me pull up. That was not an isolated experience on the journey. I am often heard before I am seen.

What a delightful visit I had with Shane and with Helen Teske, the Praise and Worship leader for Connections. ***I just missed the chance to meet Kylon Gienger, the Youth Pastor, who they told me was all of nineteen years old. The list of their "staff" is quite extensive and the vast majority of them are volunteers. The entire staffing and programming here is unique in many ways and yet highly effective. Clearly the emphasis is on outreach to and through youth.***

I loved one highlight that Shane and Helen shared with me, which involves a "blessing" on youth when they turn 16. They had one scheduled soon for sixteen young people and eleven of them were not members! In fact, nearly half of their regular attendees are not members. They also have a youth band which travels to conduct weeks of prayer in other locations

They do a lot of outreach to homeless in the community and they are planning to build a "Habitat" home. The elders truly function as elders and do a lot of prayer and visitation. They also have a strong prayer ministry as well as active men's and women's ministries.

As with most contemporary and creative worship groups they frequently undergo scrutiny and can test the boundaries related to finances, membership, and many traditions. All I can say is that I found at Connections another group of very alive, very committed, and very Christlike people and programs. I pray that church leadership will always strive to find ways to engage and incorporate new ways of reaching today's lost.

I wanted to meet next with Harry Sharley, Sr. Pastor at the 35th St. Church, which is the mother church in Yakima. Connections was a plant that came from this church about four years ago. Harry was tied up with other appointments and we only got to chat on the phone. ***While the 35th St. Church is much more traditional by comparison they are, at the same time, very supportive and encouraging regarding the ministry at Connections. Harry does not see it as a competition, but rather as a broader means of reaching more people for the kingdom. How I wish we had that attitude more often where we encounter differing worship and outreach styles.***

It was good to at least talk with Harry for a bit. We pastored together in the Potomac Conference for several years and, in fact, he was my pastor for a short time when I worked in the conference office and had my membership at the Waynesboro, Virginia Church. God bless you Harry. Keep the faith!

COULEE DAM, WASHINGTON

Now I was going to have a short break. From Yakima I headed toward Coulee Dam to spend the night with my nephew, Rick King, his wife Jamie, and son and daughter, Skylar and Ciera. Again I was riding through highways of nostalgia, especially as I stopped to visit the Ginkgo Petrified Forest near the city of Vantage. This is a beautiful spot, as well as one that brought back so many boyhood memories. The view is spectacular as it overlooks the Wanapum Reservoir on the Columbia River. Later on I also stopped at Steamboat Rock and Dry Falls State Parks. Dry Falls is thought to be the largest waterfall on record at its time, being ten times larger than Niagra Falls. It is always an impressive site to visit.

A little over 150 miles from Yakima I arrived at my nephew's home near Coulee Dam, where Rick and Jamie are both physical therapists. I always have loved Coulee Dam. I can remember when you could walk across or drive across and look over the edge as torrents of water cascaded down the spillway. Now you can't go across it and there is a mere trickle of water to view. It is still a very impressive structure. It was good to have some down time and to be with family. The big thrill was that on Friday Rick and Skylar and I would ride together over the North Cascades Pass. That was a ride I have been dreaming about for many years.

NORTH CASCADES PASS, WASHINGTON

Friday morning Rick went to do some hospital rounds and about 8:30 the two of them started up their BMW's while I provided the proper acoustics for a bike ride. What a gorgeous day it was as we headed through Coulee Dam and up Hwy 155 toward Omak and then picked up Hwy 20 toward Winthrop. We stopped in Winthrop, an absolutely delightful old west town, for a fabulous breakfast for which we were more than ready after nearly 100 miles of really fun curvy roads!

After that great meal we had the most spectacular ride of the entire trip. I had already seen a lot of wonderful country and had ridden some very special highways, particularly in Tennessee and Virginia, but this was amazing! If you are reading this and have never gone over the North Cascades Pass I want to encourage you to put it on your bucket list.

Rick and Skylar rode with me for probably another 75 miles before they turned back and I went on to Bellingham for the night. It seemed that the view just continued to outdo itself every corner we turned. The lakes we could see down below were emerald green from glacier melt and the smell of the sun on the warm pine needles was intoxicating. In short, this was a great day with two great riding buddies.

BELLINGHAM, WASHINTON

As I pulled into Bellingham, Washington for the night I was full of so many mixed emotions. It had been a breathtaking day and I was so grateful for it. Bellingham was where I had gone to college for four years and worked in a variety of places and that evoked so many memories, some good and some very bad. I was looking forward to being in the Aldergrove, B.C. Church in the morning, but most of all I was less than a week away from home and it was no longer calling me. It was screaming for me. I had ridden 10, 285 miles so far and some of my most highly anticipated stops were yet before me, but I was surely longing for Ingrid and home.

Thus ended the fifth week of the ride. Sabbath was sweet and I was looking forward to tomorrow and the last week's ride down the west coast.

Chapter the Tenth

The Fifth Decade

Shortly after my fortieth birthday our oldest son left to go to Japan as a student missionary. This was not a big surprise to us as he had spent several years in Asia and was very involved in the various Asian clubs at Pacific Union College in Angwin, California. Before he left he informed us of some of the rules related to student missionary activities. They were not to date each other. Well, knowing our son I thought that was going to be an interesting challenge, but he proved to play by the rules. In fact he played very strictly by the rules. The rules did not specifically say that he couldn't date his boss, the director of the English Language School at Harajuku, a part of Tokyo.

We began to get letters telling us about his growing friendship and we would occasionally get to talk on the phone. About eight months into the year we finally made the statement that if anything significant was going to happen at the end of the year it might be nice to know so that we could plan accordingly. Well, that did it. We soon were informed that there would be a wedding in August of 1987 and yours truly would be doing the honors. They also wanted Oma, that's Ingrid's mom, who has lived with us for nearly our entire ministry, to make the wedding cake. Of course wedding cakes, like we think of them, are not customary in Japan so we would need to bring a few things and oh, by the way, could we get the tuxedos and dresses and be sure to bring enough cake mixes and you might want to bring the pots and pans needed and would it be possible to bring the nuts and mints and anything else you think might be helpful! Oh my, this was going to be fun, and interesting!

So we packed up. There were five in our party going over as we took Susie Grindley along with us for our daughter, Julie, to have company. Susie was a friend from our time in Bozeman, Montana. Everyone was told they could have one suitcase for clothing and personal items. The other suitcase was for "stuff."

We hauled five tuxes, five bridesmaid dresses and the shoes, thirty-six boxes of cake mix and the frosting, all the pans needed, forty pounds of nuts and mints and I don't even remember what all else and off we went to Tokyo.

Arriving three days before the wedding we met our daughter-in-law, Shihoko, for the first time and it was love at first sight. Never mind jet lag, there was no time for that. The next couple of days were spent at the Tokyo Central Seventh-day Adventist Church baking and decorating cakes, which had to be baked one sheet at a time in the limited oven space. We worked hard those few days, but the wedding was a grand success and everything turned out beautifully. We had so much fun with Shihoko's parents, Chieko and Koji and her brother, Tetsu. We truly became an international family of greater proportions.

Danny and Shihoko continued to live and work in Japan for eight years before moving to the U.S. with their daughter, Lauren, and then adding our grandson, Daniel. We have been blessed by all of our children and grandchildren!

I'll never forget coming through customs in Los Angeles on the way home. The inspector wanted to know what we had purchased in Japan or Hong Kong and we told him we had not purchased anything. He looked at our ten suitcases and said, "You went all the way to Japan and didn't bring anything back with you?" We explained that we had lived in Asia for six years and didn't need any more souvenirs, but he wanted to know what was in the suitcases. We told him about the wedding and the cake and the tuxes and dresses, but I think his middle name was Thomas like mine. He told us to open up the suitcases. After about the third suitcase full of pots and pans and wedding clothes he just shook his head and waved us through.

We came back to Bozeman and did another wedding, on a much smaller scale mind you, and then left for northern Virginia where we had just accepted a call to pastor the church in Vienna, Virginia, just sixteen miles from the White House.

This was certainly a very big change for all of us. I had only visited the east coast once and to live this close to the nation's capitol was a very interesting and rewarding experience. The Vienna Church sits in a prime location with Vienna Junior Academy on the adjacent property. All of us wish we had enjoyed the beauty and quiet of Montana for a longer period, but we were excited about being back in a larger metropolitan area. The transition from Hong Kong to Montana had been significant to say the least. It also became quite obvious to us that God was actively providing for our needs.

When we went back to Vienna from Bozeman to interview we also took time to look around the area to see what housing options were like. We had not purchased a home since returning from Hong Kong and so we were looking for available rentals. I was quite concerned to see that the average three bedroom home was renting for between $1200 and $1500 per month and had serious doubts that we would be able to afford that. We knew that this was going to take some serious prayer.

Ingrid told me that she began praying immediately that God would give us a home large enough to entertain in and with enough yard to enjoy. She wanted it to be in a quiet neighborhood and she told God that we needed to have it for $500 a month or less.

When she told me her prayer it was hard for me to suppress my laughter, explaining to her that her request was so far out of the price range that it would be difficult even for God to do that. I suggested that she pray for a good paying job knowing that wages were higher here than in Montana and I hoped that God could help make up the difference in that way. She told me to pray my prayer if I wanted to, but that she would continue to pray hers, thank you very much.

You already know how this is going to turn out don't you? All the way across the country as we moved out I was concerned about where we were going to live. We would stay in a motel for a few nights, but would have to locate housing quickly. Well, the day after we arrived in

Vienna we had a phone call from a member who knew of a house that was vacant. It belonged to a lady who was in an assisted living facility in the south and the house was in the hands of an attorney. He wasn't really interested in renting the place, but he did need for the property to be cared for, as it could not be sold until she passed away. When he learned that there was a new pastor in the area needing a house he agreed to meet us. As he met Ingrid and her mother, Hanna, he was willing to strike an offer. We could move into the house on a month-to-month basis with the understanding that when the owner died we would be given thirty days notice. We could also give thirty days notice at any time. The house was a pre-Civil War estate on forty acres bordering an equestrian training center. It had a large living room, library, dining area and a large kitchen. It had three main bedrooms plus servant's quarters and the rental price…well, there was no actual rent, but we would have to pay the $450 a month for property taxes.

We lived there for over four years until I was asked to serve as Ministerial Director for the Potomac Conference and would need to move to Staunton, Virginia. When I called the attorney to let him know of our intentions he told me that he had a note on his agenda for the day to call me and let me know that the owner of the house had passed away and he was going to give us thirty days notice. Through all of this Ingrid would only smile at my weak faith. God is so good!

The Vienna years were good years. We made so many good friends in the church, many of whom remain very close friends today. We enjoyed exploring the D.C. area and also enjoyed access to the General Conference. It was during this time, however, that I began to really sense that my growing understanding of righteousness by faith and assurance of salvation was not embraced by everyone. I also sensed very different views as to what constituted a "proper" worship style.

In my previous years of ministry there had been opposition from strong-minded members at times. You may recall earlier my confrontation in my very first district. However, in Vienna I experienced differing opinions on a new level. Here, not only my methodology was brought into question, but also my theology. They even took the step of calling a meeting with the conference officers and I was definitely under attack.

Whenever anything like this comes about I realize the need to listen carefully and not just react defensively. There is the need to evaluate the concerns and criticisms being expressed to see if I have indeed gone too far. I'm not going to go into the various aspects of the theological debate that was going on here. Those who know my ministry know by now that I lean very strongly on the message of grace and assurance. My own life and background demonstrate that truly accepting Christ results in dramatic changes in lifestyle and attitudes, but I make it very clear that those changes are indeed results and have absolutely no merit on their own. Another passion of mine is to help believers realize that having accepted Christ as Savior they now HAVE eternal life and nobody can take it away from them. They can turn and deny Christ, but if they will endure, they have the absolute assurance of their salvation. For some reason there are many who don't accept that gift and somehow believe that they have to keep working and doing and achieving and overcoming in order to be saved. They won't be lost for thinking that, but they will be unhappy, joyless Christians and they often seem to take delight in making other people unhappy as well.

The problem with those who feel "called" to correct leadership is that they can bring great discouragement and they certainly did in my case. For the first time I found myself seriously depressed to the point of making a genuine attempt to leave ministry. I created and incorporated HELP, Inc. (Health Education Lifestyle Programs) and was able to obtain contracts with a few government and corporate agencies for smoking cessation and stress management programs. When a comfortable level of contracts had been made I met with my Conference and Union Presidents, Ralph Martin and Ron Wisbey. I shared my frustration and hurt and informed them of my plans. I'll never forget the look of pain on their faces. It was not that anyone was irreplaceable; rather it was that they genuinely hated to see anyone feel that vocal detractors were forcing them out.

God began to really work on my heart over the following few days and nights. There was absolutely no peace with my decision and it became clear that I was making a mistake and was taking things into my own hands rather than surrendering to His. I called Elder Martin and told him that God had changed my heart and asked him to disregard our earlier conversation. I have been privileged to work with some great leaders through my years of ministry and Ralph Martin is one of the most loving, encouraging, and sensitive men in my ministry. He understood completely and simply expressed his delight and told me not to give it another thought. And who would have thought that Ron Wisbey, another leader of the same caliber, would one day serve as the Head Elder in my church. I have been blessed!

I continued to serve in the Vienna Church for another two years and have always been so thankful that God helped me to work through that whole experience. It certainly made me more sensitive to the challenges that many of my colleagues faced. Ralph Martin then asked if I would be interested in having an intern work with me. Of course the answer was yes, and even more so learning that it was Leo Ranzolin Jr. that they were suggesting. I had met Leo at the last campmeeting and had been impressed with his friendliness and was excited about the possibility. It was surprising to learn that things were not going really well in the placement he was currently in and they wanted to see if he could be helped by working with someone else.

Leo and Susan and their two children came to Vienna and we had nothing but a great time. It became clear to me that the only problem had been a lack of determination to match skills with needs and opportunities. Leo had grown up in ministry with his father, Leo Ranzolin Sr. being a successful pastor and leader of youth all the way to the General Conference level. Leo Jr. had spent all of his life being involved in very large churches and suddenly, out of seminary, he found himself pastoring a district of very small rural churches and he simply had no idea how to work with it. This illustrates, in my mind, a trend that we see far too often. We tend to take young men and women and put them through a standardized initiation to ministry and it is usually configured to meet conference needs whether it fits the individual's gift mix or not. I believe we have lost many gifted young workers and probably injured and perhaps crippled many more. There is, of course, the need to expose new workers to a variety of experiences and I also realize the need to fill existing vacancies. However, we need to take adequate time to match gifts and personalities and backgrounds with those needs and we desperately need ministerial directors and experienced colleagues who will come alongside and mentor these interns. Looking at my own internship experience it is somewhat of a marvel that I survived.

It was during this period of time that I faced a serious health challenge as well. Having continued to run after we had returned from mission service, I ran a number of marathons in the U.S. While in Montana I ran in Billings, MT, Portland, OR, and Coeur d' Alene, Idaho. After moving to Vienna there was a marathon in Baltimore and the Marine Corps Marathon in D.C. It was also my privilege to have run Boston three times and I still consider that to be the highlight of my running memories.

One hot and humid summer afternoon I was mowing the two acres of lawn that we had and obviously was perspiring heavily. On the property adjoining ours there were a number of horses which we always enjoyed watching. This particular day the horse flies were in abundance and they were biting me through my t-shirt. When I finished there were about twenty red welts across my back and chest, but by the next day they were gone.

About two weeks later I began to feel ill and had the worst headaches in my memory. I was taking Tylenol and eventually even was given a prescription for Tylenol with codeine, but nothing would touch the headache. We had tickets to see "Fiddler On the Roof" at the Wolf Trap Foundation for the Performing Arts. We went, but I don't remember much of the program. The next day I woke up vomiting clear fluids and was completely dysfunctional. Ingrid took me to the hospital and the next four days are totally blank to me. She told me that twice during that time my survival was in question. Finally the diagnosis came in of viral encephalitis.

There is always a humorous side to things if we look for it. Our daughter, Julie, was attending Shenandoah Valley Academy and was quite distraught as she shared with her friends and teachers the need to pray for her dad who had viral syphilis. Thankfully the faculty checked it out before they shared the news!

Obviously, recovery did come over the following several weeks and I even ran Boston one more time. However, about two months after that last marathon I began to experience some constriction in my joints. I found it difficult to put my foot up on the car bumper to tie my shoes. Eventually this problem got to the point where I was having difficulty walking, getting in and out of a car, and even dressing. After going through seemingly unending tests and trials they put the name of Reiter's Syndrome on it and started a regimen of heavy doses of Prednisone with all of the expected side effects. However, it did allow me to move again.

Now, many years later I am off of Prednisone and all other meds as well, but never was able to return to running at a level that would allow me to complete marathons. The good news is that there is life after running! God is good and I do enjoy good health although my immune system doesn't seem to be as strong since the encephalitis. Ah well, Jesus will make all things right one day!

About the same time that all of this was taking place I had the opportunity and extreme privilege of serving as the Ministerial Director for the Potomac Conference. This was after four and a half years at the Vienna Church and I left there at a positive time.

I truly loved my five years as the "Rev's Rev". That was my customized license plate. I'll never forget the first day of this new assignment, however. We were still living in Vienna for the first several months of transition. While driving down to Staunton, Virginia for my inaugural day I left with great excitement, but getting closer and closer to the conference office I became more and more uncertain about what to expect.

When walking into the office building there was no one to greet me. I said hello to the receptionist, who recognized me as one of the pastors, but I don't think she knew of my new responsibilities. I walked through the double doors into the office hallway knowing that my new office was to the right, but instead turned left into the office of Dave Anderson, one of the assistant treasurers for the conference. We sat and talked for over an hour before I got up the courage to go to my office and greet my secretary, Merry Knoll.

There had been no job description given as yet and I was actually pretty uncertain as to what was supposed to be done other than be a support to the pastors in their various churches and districts. Finally Elder Ralph Martin, the conference president, invited me into his office and we just talked for a while. He said that he thought I had probably thought about this kind of opportunity for some time and he was right. If there was one position in the level of administration that held any interest for me, this was it. Elder Martin then told me that my assignment was to simply follow my dream and then after a year we would evaluate how that was going. That, my friends, is a pretty amazing job description! That told me that he had a lot of trust and confidence in me and I will forever be grateful for it.

I simply began to visit as many pastors as possible and get familiar with their needs. My main task was being an encourager and supporter. I well remember one day that first week when Merry handed me a copy of my predecessor's last newsletter. Not being the kind of communicator that likes putting together and organizing a newsletter, my mind began searching for an alternate way. I have always found newsletters to be out of date by the time they arrive. Mind you, Dan Goddard, who had served here before me and left to return to pastoring in Frederick, Maryland, was an amazing pastor to the pastors. He had stood by my side during challenging days in Vienna and I aspired to be as effective as he was, but still didn't like newsletters. So, I decided to just write a letter to the pastors describing my feelings and reactions to the change I was undergoing and assuring them of my desire to help them if there was any way that could happen. I threw in a little humor, which those who know me will not be surprised to hear, and got quite a few positive responses to that letter. The next week I did the same thing and thus was born the VIP, a weekly letter to Very Important Pastors. I kept that up for five years and still get comments about some of those epistles. That same approach has continued to be effective in the local church, now to Very Important Parishioners. In Napa I just wrote VIP #554, and haven't missed a week of sending out this two-page communication. It has proven to be one of the most effective things I have done in ministry.

Through these five years I loved my contact with and ministry to a wide variety of pastors. We worked through some challenges, but we also had a lot of fun. Eventually I also carried most of the responsibility for personnel although everything was subject to the input and approval of conference leadership. In this capacity there came the privilege of building some very close friendships with a number of men and women as we worked through changes in placement and as I sought to bring in new pastors to our field. Many of these friendships remain very close yet today.

I believe that the position of Ministerial Director is one that is vital to the spiritual health of our pastors. They need someone who will listen without judging and in confidentiality. They need someone who has the ear of conference administration when a change is needed. Every pastor needs a pastor. In these days of financial challenges and downsizing the position of Ministerial Director is most often either cut or melded with other responsibilities. I think this is a huge mistake. I can most clearly speak just for myself. There are many times when I need to be ministered to with no agenda other than loving concern.

There are so many stories from these wonderful years, but I'll spare you. During this time I had the joy of co-authoring two books with Len McMillan. We wrote "First-Class Male" in 1994 and "Putting Up With Mr. Right" in 1996. I also began to enjoy the opportunity to speak at a wide variety of Pastor's Retreats, Men's Retreats, Couple's Retreats, and other gatherings. In 1995 Len McMillan, Lynn Schlisner, and myself, along with our wives and some of our children all went to Utrecht, Holland for the end of the General Conference there and picked up an ADRA van and drove through Germany, Poland, the Czech Republic, and Slovakia. In Slovakia we all shared together in a retreat for the pastors in that conference. What a privilege it was to minister to them. We had some interesting, and harrowing, experiences as all nine of us packed into that nine passenger, non-air-conditioned, clunker and drove through the summer heat and humidity. We lost the transmission in Germany, but just happened to be where Ingrid's family lived and one of her cousins had it repaired in no time. We lost the brakes coming down a hill in the Czech Republic in the middle of nowhere, but coasted around the corner and found a brand new Ford dealership just waiting to repair the brakes on this Ford van. I keep telling you, God is so good!

I have nothing but wonderful memories of my time as the Rev's Rev. There were beginning to be some inquiries as to my interest in serving as conference secretary in other conferences. I went through one interview process and had to do some serious thinking as to what God wanted me to do and some serious praying as well. I clearly began to sense God calling me back to the local church to resume my ministry in that capacity. I had just turned the big Five-O and was waiting for God to open just the right door. Then things got interesting. I'll see you in chapter twelve.

Chapter the Eleventh

The Sixth Week

Last night I was just too tired to tour around Bellingham to see what had changed since I went to college there over forty years ago. I knew I would have some free time on my way back from Aldergrove, B.C. It was exciting to get on my way there on this beautiful and sunny Sabbath morning. I also was not exactly sure how things might have changed in the border crossing process and wanted to give myself a little extra wiggle room on the time.

ALDERGROVE, BRITISH COLUMBIA, CANADA

It is a short ride from Bellingham out the Guide Meridian Road to the Aldergrove Border Crossing. Going north the line was quite short and I zipped through. They only asked a few questions after showing them my passport, which you now must have to journey into Canada, and I was now in Canadian territory. From the crossing it is a straight shot just 7 km to the church. The thing that disturbed me was the very long line of cars waiting the cross into the U.S. and wondered how long that was going to take on my way back.

The Aldergrove Church is a beautiful facility and very people friendly. I quickly found the Associate Pastor, Francis Douville, who has been there for over five years. The Lead Pastor, Dave Jamieson, was out of town, but Francis was very helpful in giving me a quick tour of the facility and chatting with me for a while.

This church is unique and alive and they don't have an extremely contemporary service. The book membership is around 600 and they have over 500 in attendance in their two worship services. I attended the first service, which did have a group leading praise songs, but it was all very mellow. In the second service they pick up the pace a bit, but it is still not nearly as contemporary as many churches I visited. ***The average age of their congregation is around 30. So what are they doing?***

I would say that my first impression was that this church belonged to the people. Pr. Francis took me down the stairs to the children's divisions. I was amazed at the painting on all of the walls depicting children in all parts of the world. The painting was professional in quality and the faces on the children were the actual faces of the children from the church. It was fantastic!

One of the keys to the effectiveness of this church family is the amount of activity going on that they can be involved in. Aldergrove has a program simply called AOK (Acts Of Kindness). ***Some of the activities are quick and simple and some are very complex and detailed. Every***

year, since 2004, they have undertaken an Extreme Home Repair for a family in need. They have a program to provide free oil changes for single moms. They provide daily breakfasts for the kids at one elementary school and weekly dinners for individuals in need. There are special dinners at Christmas for up to 150 people along with gifts for the children. They have provided four refurbished vans for single moms with cars that are on their last legs and they also run CHIP programs and cooking schools. In short, they are an extremely active, social, enterprising body of Christ and everyone seems to have a part in the program somewhere. ***If I had to choose one church, out of the seventy that I came in contact with, this would be the one I would hold up as a model. They are contemporary and up to date in programming, appearance, and vision. They partner with local and province wide agencies in order to do a greater work and they utilize everyone who wants to be involved. You would do well to look them up on the internet at aldergrovesda.org.***

After the first service I was talking with one of the elders and I mentioned the long lines leading to the border crossing. "Ah," he said, "I'll tell you a secret. Go down to 8th street and turn left. Go one mile and turn right and go another mile to 1st street. Turn right again and in one mile you'll be at the border crossing. From there you can merge into the line and save one mile of traffic." Bingo, it worked like a charm and with the bike it was particularly easy. I was back in the USA in less than thirty minutes!

I came back into Bellingham and did some riding around as I looked up places I had worked and lived and then drove up through Western Washington University Campus. It was simply a time of reminiscing. Surprisingly much of it looked the same. It is amazing how fast time slips away. I moved to Bellingham in 1964 and left in 1969. Forty years had gone by…FAST!

Well, enough for flashbacks, it was time to move on. Rather than get back on I-5 I took the scenic route down Chuckanut Drive. This is truly one of the most beautiful rides in the northwest. The trick is to just take it slow and breathe in the beauty. It is only a little over 20 miles long and it comes out in Burlington after passing through such hamlets as Edison and Bow.

Now I joined with I-5 and headed to a birthday celebration for Frank Jorgensen. My arrival there would be a surprise to him, but the rest of the family knew I was coming. Frank and Ursula are wonderful friends and part of a German clan that are like family to us and they are all members of the Edmonds Seventh-day Adventist Church. I was staying tonight with other very special and long-time friends, Klaus and Adele Hann. I often recognize how wonderfully blessed I am. Ingrid and I have friends and family (and sometimes it's hard to tell them apart) all over the world. When we retire I think we'll just travel around the world and visit each of them for just a few days and then move on. If you consider yourself a friend of mine you might want to prepare now!

We all did have a wonderful afternoon and evening and then Sunday morning I made my way over to see my sister and brother-in-law in Sequim, Washington. However, on my way I had to spend a little time in Edmonds.

Edmonds, Washington is where I grew up, and is such a lovely town, which is situated right on Puget Sound. This is a gorgeous part of the country where you can see the Olympic and the Cascade Mountain Ranges. Puget Sound is also the gateway to the San Juan Islands. It seems that beauty just surrounds you here. I stopped and walked the hallways of my former elementary school just for fun. It is now an adult education center, but I love to go back into some of the rooms I knew as a boy. I also rode past some of the other places that hold special memories including the house I spent most of my youth in. It's amazing how much smaller everything seems now.

Next I got on the Washington State Ferry that crosses the Sound from Edmonds to Kingston. I never get tired of this ride. It was so special to me as a boy. It also holds memories because the ashes from both of my parents were scattered on this stretch of water. The Washington State Ferry system offers a great service free of charge. All we had to do when my parents passed away was give them a few days' notice and they stopped the ferry in the middle of a run, blew the ship's whistle and made an announcement that there would be a scattering of ashes. They allowed us a few moments for this and then resumed the crossing. After that, the ship's captain came down with a card showing the ship's name, the latitude and longitude, the time, and his name. I think this is a wonderful gesture of respect for those who wish to remember a loved one.

Riding from Kingston to Sequim is such a beautiful journey. The sight and smell and feel of the Olympic Peninsula is very special to me and I loved this slow paced ride through forests, along coastlines, and across the Hood Canal Floating Bridge. Arriving in Sequim I stopped for a latte at my favorite coffee shop, The Buzz, and then went to see my family. Tom and Phyllis King bought the house that my parents had lived in and did a marvelous job of updating it. Their home is so warm, relaxing, and cozy that it is just a pleasure to walk in the door. Tom's mother, Clara, also lives with them and we had a great time just being together. It's amazing how Phyllis and I could fight so much as kids and love each other so much now. I don't know why we fought before, being pretty much a model brother!

While there I did get to see my nephew and his family. Lance and Jen King, with their three children, Alex, Dillon, and Ashley are just fun and the kids always love to see their "Crazy Uncle Marv." Since this visit Lance and family have moved to Montana and Tom and Phyllis have moved back over to the east side of the Sound. Sequim just won't be the same, but I'll always love it.

SEQUIM, WASHINGTON

Another thing Sequim has, besides beautiful and comparatively dry weather, is a very pretty and friendly Seventh-day Adventist Church. On Monday morning I met Pastor Dale Kongorski at the best breakfast place in the entire Northwest, the Oak Table. If you're ever in the area you simply must stop there for breakfast, but you may have to wait for a table.

The Sequim Seventh-day Adventist Church is one that I have had the privilege of attending on a number of occasions and have even preached there. In fact my sister and brother-in-law were members there. ***I always loved the Sabbath School class that met out in the Fireside Room. You were always welcome to pick up a hot or cold drink and join in a circle. Every time I attended there I was made to feel very welcome***

and included and I think that's what we all desire when we come to church isn't it?

I would describe the church, as a whole, to be quite traditional and perhaps somewhat conservative, and yet they have always demonstrated a welcome openness and inclusiveness to all who come to worship there.

Although I didn't have the opportunity to attend on this trip, Dale told me that they continue to have a really strong Sabbath School program with many choices available. However, he also shared that they have a lack of young families and that their school is facing major challenges. It would seem to me, therefore, that we simply have to be even more deliberate in not only welcoming young families, but also intentionally seeking them and providing the programming that they need for themselves and for their children.

It would only be fair to say that Sequim is definitely known as a retirement area, but I know that it is also experiencing significant growth and change. The church is going to have to be willing to participate in the changing makeup of the community if it is going to continue to be effective in sharing the gospel.

There are a significant number of health professionals in this congregation and they do participate in a strong health and medical outreach. Perhaps adding other offerings, such as parenting, financial planning, stress management, day care, or any number of other possibilities will result in new growth for this great church family that will always be special to me.

I next enjoyed the ride back to Kingston and across Puget Sound once again. I love to watch from the upper deck of the ferry as long as possible as the ship comes into the Edmonds dock. I can see all the scenes of my boyhood days. I always am able to pick out Walnut, Maple, Dayton, and Main Streets. I can spot the old Edmonds Elementary School and the building that was my Junior High School as well. My entire childhood world is laid out before me and it is beautiful.

I had an appointment with my Aunt Bonnie this morning as well and that is always a treat. This sweet lady was always so kind to me as I was growing up in a home that was not always easy. She still is kind to me! We love to visit and laugh and remember and I wish there were more opportunities to spend time with my aunts, uncle, and many cousins. Family is such a wonderful gift.

I rode to her condo, which is near the water, and left my bike there. Bonnie and I walked to her favorite coffee shop and then we walked a few blocks to the Visitor Center, where she works as a volunteer. The Visitor Center is a reconstructed log cabin that sits right next to what was the old library. I couldn't help but point out to her the lower level of that building that used to house the police station and jail where I got to spend those few hours back when I was ten years old and got caught stealing candy. That was over fifty years ago, but the memory is still very vivid!

After a tour of the center and a short visit I walked back to my aunt's condo and hopped on the bike for a leisurely ride down I-5 to spend the evening with Mike Speegle and talk about the Kelso/Longview Church.

KELSO/LONGVIEW, WASHINGTON

Mike was a pastor in Northern California before moving to Kelso/

Longview several years ago with a unique challenge of stepping into a church that was already very successful and energetic. He admits to having some qualms about that, but I can assure you that he has done well at building upon inherited success. ***I think that is a tribute to a congregation as much as to a pastor. When a church begins to really believe in themselves and in their message and their mission you just have to step in and let them run. Mike has nurtured their confidence.***

This church has, for years, put on an amazing "Walk Through Bethlehem" experience for the community. I walked with Mike through the set, which is quite impressive. Every year thousands of local residents and others from a distance come to experience this real life drama unfold. They have also added an Easter outreach. This is all in addition to a full plate of offerings for youth programs and many other more traditional outreach efforts.

This was a really fun visit. What they do here would not be easy to duplicate in other areas, but it is a niche that they have filled and it has brought them great success in reaching their community. In addition

I had a great night's rest, a wonderful meal prepared by Mike, and an opportunity to renew a friendship with a pastor for whom I have great respect.

I have to admit that I was beginning to think more and more of home by now. Napa was easily within a day's ride, but I still had appointments that I very much wanted to keep. So, Tuesday morning I left for the short ride to Gresham, Oregon. There I was looking forward to meeting with Jared Spano. We have known the Spano family since Potomac Conference days and have always loved the energy of the three boys. Jared even spent a short time as an extern for the Napa Church when he was at PUC. He later transferred to Walla Walla and was picked up by the Oregon Conference and that was a good move on their part.

GRESHAM, OREGON

The Gresham Church is average in appearance and average in the makeup of its membership. Where it goes way above average is in its love for the people who show up. ***Jared told me the story of a young man who was recently released from prison. He showed up with tattoos, a girlfriend, a baby, and a long list of needs. A lot of churches would be nice, but keep a bit of distance. This church, however, invited this young man to come and work with them. They got acquainted and made them all feel like part of the family (which in case you have forgotten, they are).***

Jared was in the middle of a sermon series based on the well known quote from Ministry of Healing, p. 143, "Christ's method alone will give true success in reaching the people. The Saviour mingled with men as one who desired their good. He showed His sympathy for them, ministered to their needs and won their confidence. Then He bade them, 'Follow Me.'"

We have seen this before and it truly is the method that will be most successful in reaching the hearts of men and women. ***It is wonderful to have state of the art facilities. It is wonderful to have a church loaded with professionals and talent. It is wonderful to have a budget that is more than ample, but if you only have Christ's love and heart for people you will build His church.***

Keep on keepin' on, Jared. We're proud of you.

Next stop was Pleasant Hill, Oregon and the home of Lane and Carrie Meadowcroft. Lane and Carrie were vital members and leaders in the Napa Church for several years of our ministry there. Job needs necessitated a move to Oregon and we mourned our loss. Friendships, however, are forever and we love every chance we get to see them.

PLEASANT HILL, OREGON

Lane and Carrie are part of the Pleasant Hill Church just a few miles east of Eugene. ***Dave McCoy is the pastor there and has been there for 16 years. Praise God for longer pastoral stays! This church has had a strong outreach to younger families and has drawn many of the students from the University of Oregon in Eugene. They will come all the way out to Pleasant Hill because of the loving atmosphere and inclusive spirit. One really neat activity that Dave shared was having the students from their Jr. Academy go to the local bank that had recently been robbed twice and they prayed all around the building, at each door, and inside. This got media attention, but more importantly, it touched the hearts of the employees. What a great way to build relationships in the community!***

One of the most effective tools of evangelism is simply to have our eyes open and our antennas up! Things happen all around our churches that create opportunities for us to respond. ***Our goal is not always to build big churches. Isn't it more important to build big relationships within our walls and out in the community?***

Staying here overnight was a real treat. Neither Lane nor Carrie was home when I arrived. The dog did a great job of welcoming me. Lane told me the house was unlocked and I was free to go in. They live on a wonderful piece of land out in the country. I opted to just sit on the patio with the dog and enjoy the peace and serenity and look forward to an evening with friends and their pastor. The next day was Wednesday and I would be home in just two days...or so I thought!

Wednesday morning I had yet another wonderful breakfast with Lane and Carrie. On my way back to I-5 I stopped to take some pictures of the church and then just enjoyed the peaceful ride down the country road. My next stop was Grants Pass. This church, too, has some special memories. We have attended there several times when Ingrid's uncle, Fred Adam, was a member, and elder, and a Sabbath School teacher there.

GRANT'S PASS, OREGON

The Grants Pass Church is a marvelous facility and has more outreach opportunity than any church its size that I have ever seen. The Sr. Pastor, Marvin Clark, was out of town, as was the Youth Pastor, Ed Nelson, but I was welcomed by two associates, Chuck Austin and Glen Chinn. Chuck is a "local hire" associate and Glen is a much valued "retired" associate. ***They even let me sit at the desk with the sign for Pr. Marvin. I felt right at home!***

Grants Pass has a very impressive TV studio operated by BLBN (Better Life Broadcasting Network), which is affiliated with 3ABN and is reaching a wide area. This ministry is bringing many new faces to the church. They are also very active with health programs such as CHIP and NEWSTART and they have a beautiful Community Service Center, Thrift Store, and meeting/fellowship hall. There is absolutely no lack of tools and facilities for outreach here. In addition they have a very active youth ministry and are working hard to include the youth in the worship service. This is truly a beautiful church! Grants Pass has a long history of successful evangelistic outreach.

Here is an example of a church with an abundant amount of tools and resources and they are using them with good results. As I mentioned in the reports from the previous two churches, however, having a heart for the people God places in your view is the most important key. It is always nice to see what can happen when you have both. Grants Pass was such a place.

What a treat was ahead of me now. I rode through Grants Pass and on to Hwy 199 toward the northern California border and Hwy 101. I could almost smell home! You have all heard the line about when the horse senses the smell of the barn...well, then you can sense what is coming.

Hwy 199 is a glorious 80 mile ride that winds through thick coastal forests and ends up merging onto Hwy 101 at Crescent City, which is always a delightful ride. I was pushing just a bit as it was already well past noon and I had another 260 miles still ahead of me before I reached Fortuna. I always have to stop at Trees of Mystery. I remember stopping there when I was seven years old and to this day I have never gone by without stopping. You just have to have a chat with Paul Bunyan!

FORTUNA, CALIFORNIA

It was late in the afternoon when I pulled into the Fortuna Church parking lot to meet with Dave Perry, who had been pastoring there only since the previous September. Fortuna is yet another church with family ties. My brother-in-law, Victor Neufeld, grew up in Fortuna as part of a rather significant German group. Now almost all of the German families have either moved away or passed on. This was a booming logging area in years past, but much of that industry has shut down. Fortuna, however, is a lovely area, especially if you like ocean front living.

As I said, Dave is fairly new here and is working hard to create new momentum in the church. Shortly after he came he convinced the leaders to switch the meeting times around and they now have worship at 10:00 and Sabbath School at 11:30. He feels that has been a successful adaptation to the needs of younger families and has resulted in a good increase in Sabbath School attendance and no loss in the worship service. Often it is good to be willing to try new approaches. You can always go back to the way it was before, but you won't know if something will work until you try it.

Dave, along with some local leaders has also presented a series of meetings that convenes on Friday evening, Sabbath morning, and Saturday evening. Dave and two others each preach a short message at each meeting and the theme is "Christ For the Common Man." The atmosphere, dress, and format is more casual and I think this is a great idea.

Since the local campmeeting was cancelled this year they also initiated a creative idea. The Red Cross Bloodmobile always came to Redwood Campmeeting and so Dave has invited them to come and set up for donations after church on Sabbath. That may have some interesting

responses, but I believe this is the kind of creativity and outreach that we need to be exploring. Keep it up, Dave.

I might just add here that we set up a Sabbath after church blood drive in Napa recently as well. It was a well received outreach and we had a great response both from church members and the community.

The original plan was to stay with Dave and Arleen that night and I was very much looking forward to getting better acquainted, but had made a call to Ingrid while gassing up just before meeting with him. We had begun to calculate that if I left Fortuna by 6:30 I could actually be home by midnight. Having already ridden 340 miles I knew that home was another 260, but couldn't resist the temptation to sleep in my own bed.

I called Paul Hawks, the Sr. Pastor of the Ukiah Church. Ukiah was scheduled to be my last stop before home and it is a very special one because that is where my spiritual journey in the Seventh-day Adventist Church began and where I was baptized. Ingrid's sister, Lilli Teichman, lives there and we visit and attend there often and consider it home in many ways. Paul had a tight schedule on Thursday and knowing I would have had to leave Fortuna early there still would only have been an hour at the most to visit. I knew I could meet with Paul easily at a later date with more time and on and on the rationalization went. I apologized to Dave for my unsocial departure. It is really Arleen that needs to be commended for her gracious understanding, but home was calling and I was answering. I called to let Ingrid know the change in plans and to leave the lights on and the dog tied up. Actually we don't have a dog, but I had been gone so long I thought she might have gotten one!

By the time Ukiah came it was already getting dark and I only stopped for gas, made a quick call to Lilli, and kept on riding. Riding through Santa Rosa, now in the dark, I almost turned the ride into a mistake. They were doing a lot of road repaving on Hwy 101. I didn't realize that one lane had been repaved and the other one had not. Switching lanes I hit that uneven ridge. That is not a problem if you are aware of it and turn into the edge, but I engaged it without an angled approach and almost lost the bike. Thank God for His care for tired, homesick, bikers! No mishaps, a prayer of thanks, and a promise to myself that I would be more observant kept me safe over the last 60 miles.

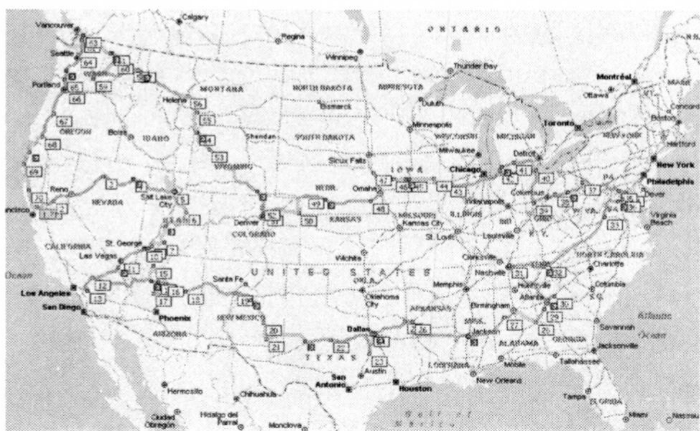

I pulled into the garage at 11:30 was greeted with a welcome home hug and kiss from Ingrid. The odometer showed that I had ridden 11,393 miles since backing the bike out of the garage. I was definitely tired from a 600 mile day, definitely glad to be home, and definitely thankful for all of God's blessings, protection, and for all the men and women I had shared with over the past many weeks. The song is so right; "Be it ever so humble, there's no place like home!"

Believe it or not, I didn't sleep in the next morning. We got up early and she went off to work. I began the long process of sorting things out and just trying to get everything put away and gathering materials together. It was good to be home and I found it hard to believe all that had been experienced over the past seven weeks. I was extremely aware of and thankful for God's blessings and protection, with no accidents, no mechanical trouble, no health issues, and very little bad weather.

I was now faced with balancing the work of writing, editing, and publishing along with re-entry into the needs of a large congregation. It has taken longer than I thought it would and I appreciate the patience and encouragement of my wife and my church. I have done a lot of reflection regarding the conversations and observations experienced. What is my perception of the health of our churches across this Division? I'll wrap that all up in the final chapter.

Before I close this chapter, however, I still have to make up the visit with Paul Hawks and since I am at this moment recovering from a back surgery I am going to do it by phone while my plan was to ride up for the visit.

UKIAH, CALIFORNIA

There is so very much to share about this precious church. This is where we were living when I went to that Heritage Singers Concert way back in 1971 and gave my life into the hands of God and my life changed forever, in fact, for eternity!

The church membership at that time just took me and loved me into the church and I pretty well covered that back in chapter six so I won't go through all those details again, but Ukiah will always seem to be my "Home Church". This is where I was baptized. This is where the membership encouraged and supported me in my ministerial preparation. This is the church that has always taken an interest in our ministry and loved us and we love them back.

Ukiah is unique in that it is a relatively small town. The population within the city limits is less than 16,000 and yet the church membership stands at over 600 and has been much higher in the past. There is an Adventist Hospital in the town, which is highly respected, and there have always been a large number of medical professionals in the church family.

As times have changed so has the environment. The Adventist Hospital is now in a newer facility, but as is the case in many of our denominationally sponsored hospitals, there are often more non-church members employed than members. This change in the makeup of hospital staffing also impacts the church in membership and finances.

Ukiah Junior Academy is one of the few schools I am aware of that still operates on the Temple Plan. This means that every student is able to attend tuition free and the local church supports fully the financial needs of the school. As membership numbers and makeup change there is the obvious reflection in the support of the school finances and the upkeep of a large and beautiful church facility.

Keeping up with changing circumstances, changing needs, changing methodologies and the necessity of therefore changing our approaches is a huge challenge to any church.

Ukiah has endeavored, through the years, to offer a variety of worship opportunities to meet the needs of the larger family. For many years there has been a group that meets in the Youth Chapel early on Sabbath mornings from 8:20 – 9:15. Their music is better described as Southern Gospel, or "Gaither" style. Interestingly this group that was once perceived as a younger generation offering is now attended mostly by those in their 50's +! Their music may have been contemporary when they started, but it isn't any more! Paul shared with me that about 75% of them stay on for Sabbath School and Church as well.

There is now a more contemporary group that meets in the same Youth Chapel twice a month on Friday nights. They are simply called, "Connect," and the interest is growing among families with children.

Ukiah has many of the more traditional outreach programs and they have conducted a large number of evangelistic series through the years and continue to do so. They have a very active, and very nice, Community Service Center that mainly focuses on clothing needs.

A large number of members actively distribute GLOW (Giving Light to Our World) tracts to homes or leaving them in public places as a means of creating interests. The church also sponsors Depression Recovery classes and other health related programs.

One big event for the whole community occurs each December with their annual Christmas Cantata, which is offered on the first or second Sunday in December and involves individuals from many churches in the community and some who are not involved with any church. The program is shared twice on the given day and the attendance is always between 800 and 1,000, with most being from the community.

One new program Paul is hoping to offer is "Ten Great Dates Before You Say I Do." This is based on a book published by Zondervan. There is a great follow-up to that in, "Ten Great Dates To Energize Your Marriage." I believe that these are the kinds of offerings we need to bring to the community to meet current needs. Then we can work on sharing Jesus and the wonderful message we have.

So, what can I say about this church so very dear to my heart?

The number of active members is lower by far now than it was when I joined the church there. There are a number of creative attempts to reach new young families, but these efforts are not always given a priority of support. The church, the school, and the people are aging and finances are a bigger challenge than they used to be. Where do we go from here?

And with that question nagging my mind I complete the circuit of this great land and the many churches I connected with. Yes, there were so many visits, so many challenges, so many opportunities, so many obstacles, and so many differing circumstances and yet so much the same. There is an answer. There is but one answer. That answer is so simple…simply Jesus. We must take our eyes off of each other and off of what is in our path and surrender everything, and I mean absolutely everything, to Jesus. We are His children and this is His church. If He were to walk among us today He would connect with those seeking Him with whatever means would reach them.

Jesus today would blog, twitter, text, and podcast. At the same time He would sit and give simple Bible studies to any who would listen and who wanted to learn. He would leave no stone unturned and no person would be turned away who wanted to be in His service. My heart is so full, but I must move on to the conclusion of this book.

Chapter the Twelth

The Sixth Decade

When we last talked, I had just turned 50 and was feeling God's leading to return to active pastoring. I had enjoyed every day of serving as Ministerial Director in the Potomac Conference and believe that we shared the love and respect of at least most of the pastors. We did have a lot of fun and I did my best to minister to them. But, administration was not a calling that really tugged at my heart and I missed having my own church family.

I had always held an admiration for Phil Dunham, who had served in the Oregon Conference as a Departmental Director during my time there. On two different occasions he took positions in the conference office and then would return to local pastorates. God has assured us that He gives different gifts to each one and at least one to each person. Some of our leaders truly have the gift of administration and I have been blessed to work with many of them. I have also seen some who took office roles and never looked back and probably should have. Too often there is a perception that serving in the conference office is a "promotion." It is not. It is a privilege to serve wherever God leads and we surely need gifted administrators at all levels, but the front line is the front line and I guess I'm a soldier and not a General.

There began to be some conversations with the conferences in California. Our real reason for wanting to go that direction was related to family, although we were in a "no-win" situation there. We have children and grandchildren on both coasts, but both of Ingrid's sisters live in northern California and we had spent our entire ministry outside of that area. She had followed me and supported my ministry for twenty-seven years and it was time to put her first in our choice of location if God would see fit to open a door.

I was not looking for any particular size in a church, but only wanted a church that wanted to have some fun, grow, and share the gospel. The direction seemed to lead to the Southern California Conference. I began having conversations with Dan Savino Sr., Director of the West Region for that area. There were a couple of churches that were looking for pastors and we finally agreed to come out and meet with the church leadership in Ventura, which is certainly a beautiful setting right on the Pacific Ocean.

Ingrid and I flew out in the Fall of 1996 and met with the Board of Elders. We talked for some time and they shared that their previous pastor had been there for just over ten years. Keith Mulligan had served well and successfully and was much loved. I took all of those as good signs. They told me that they were looking for someone who could move them even further forward from there and those were the magic words. This seemed like a match made in Heaven and we were excited about the opportunity.

Once again Ingrid was left with most of the hard work of preparing for the move and she also faced the challenge of gaining employment, hopefully being able to continue with the denomination in order to keep her retirement going. Those were large, and unfair, challenges for her, but she did it once again. She was able to work in the Pacific Union Office in Westlake Village as part of the PlusLine team. She did enjoy that work very much and was able to make a lot of friends around the Division through that position.

What happened next in Ventura is hard to explain and painful to recall. Within a few weeks it became clear to me that the wishes and thoughts and support of the Board of Elders did not necessarily reflect the thinking of the church as a whole. As I recall it was only about three or four weeks into my ministry there that an anonymous letter was circulated giving serious question to my theology. From that point on it seemed to me that everything we tried to do was met with opposition, mostly from hidden sources.

I'm not going to go into detail here and I am going to take as much responsibility for all that happened there as anyone. All that is certain is that I began to feel very unfulfilled, frustrated, and began to suffer from some significant depression that got to a pretty dangerous level.

One of the great hazards of ministry is not being honest with yourself when things are not going well regardless of whose fault it is. We usually feel the need, as pastors, to be upbeat and positive. When that requires us to put up a false front for an extended period of time, things can go downhill pretty fast. It impacts our relationships, our health, and our ministry. Many, if not most, of us find it hard to reach out and even harder to admit to ourselves how bad things really are. I thank God for a few supportive and caring friends and especially for a patient and loving wife.

While we still have some ongoing very close friendships with some of the members from Ventura the overall experience was very painful and I am extremely thankful to God that He provided an opportunity for us to try again. God then led us from our most challenging pastoral experience to our most rewarding one. Perhaps there were indeed some things I needed to learn in preparation for where we are today.

Strangely enough we had been approached to put our names on the list for the Napa Church two years previously. We had only been in Ventura for a year at that time and although we were beginning to really feel the struggle there we didn't feel that we should consider a move at that time. I'm sure it is in the best interest of every person involved that things worked out the way they did. We stayed in Ventura for two more years and Jim Pedersen moved from the Eagle Rock Church to take the Napa Church.

At that time the Napa congregation was going through some major challenges related to music and worship style and I don't need to go into all of that and I'm sure I don't understand it well enough to present it fairly anyway. Over the two year period that Jim was in Napa he led the church through some rough water and put it on a steady course. That was not without some pain. There were many families that chose to move their membership from Napa to other churches and that is always a hard experience for a church family. After two years there Jim had an opportunity to move into the conference office as the Assistant to the President, Darold Retzer. Since that time he served as Conference Secretary and for the past four years he has been my Conference President and, I might add, a member of our church in Napa, as well as simply a good friend.

Now that Napa was open again we were contacted and asked if we would consider it once again. Interestingly the Napa church had already interviewed four other pastors, had invited each of them, with unanimous votes, to take the leadership role, and had each candidate choose not to accept. I guess when they couldn't find anyone else to talk to they contacted us;>)

So, here we had a church that had gone through some serious pain interviewing a pastor who had gone through some serious pain. That's pretty interesting, don't you think? My attitude at that point was that I was tired of playing games. I was not about to go up there and try to impress them in order to get an invitation but was determined to simply be myself, be honest, and let the chips fall where they may. It was not my intention to come across as arrogant, but I did want to be transparent. If they needed somebody to referee disputes and lay out what the standards and lifestyle of a Christian should be they probably should keep looking. I was called to bring people into a saving relationship with Jesus Christ and then lead by example, but let Him do the changing and directing in their lives.

We met with the church board and spent a little over an hour going over many of the usual and customary banter. I shared a brief sketch of our ministry experience and our backgrounds. They asked some of the expected questions and I suspected that some were trying to determine where I was on the conservative/liberal spectrum. Then they asked if I had any thoughts as to how I might begin a ministry in Napa. Looking around the room my comment was that I would hope that we could change some of the makeup of the board as there was only one person that appeared to be anywhere near 40. There was a little more dialogue and we were free to return to our motel room. I recall saying to Ingrid as we walked to the car, "I don't think I'd take that church if they did offer it to me." We had, however, already agreed to speak in Napa that Sabbath.

Elder Retzer called later that evening and said that there had been a lot of discussion and that they had indeed invited us to serve the Napa Church. I could hear some concern in his voice as he shared with me that the vote had not been unanimous. "In fact," he said, "it was 14 – 5." My response was, "Good! That means that they were listening and thinking." I also shared that we would go ahead and attend and speak on Sabbath, but that I would not make a final binding decision until there was a chance to meet with the whole church rather than just the board. I had learned that lesson the hard way in Ventura.

I shared the sermon that I consider to be my "trademark" message. The title of that sermon is "Holding the Ropes." I tell of the young paralytic being lowered down into the presence of Jesus as told in Luke 5:17-19. Listeners are asked to imagine that they are the man on the stretcher, so conspicuously placed in the midst of the crowd of people. Then they are asked what they see as they are lowered into the room. They tell me of the people, of Jesus, of the hole in the roof, and then finally of the faces of the friends who had held their ropes so that they could be placed in the presence of Jesus. I ask them, "Who has held your ropes so that you could remain in the presence of Jesus?"

Next we go to Acts, first in chapter seven as Saul holds the garments of those who stone Stephan and then on to chapter nine as he sets out to Damascus to persecute the followers of "The Way." Jesus ambushes Saul and brings about one of the most spectacular conversions in the entire Bible. Saul becomes Paul and he begins to preach with power that Jesus is indeed the Christ. The Jews are determined to kill him and they watch the city gates, but men chosen by God lower Paul over the wall in a basket and as a result we have half of our New Testament. And now the question is, "Who is in your basket? Because just as surely as others have held your ropes, so God has placed people in your basket."

When God places individuals in our basket our only task is to hold their ropes. He does not ask us to judge them, measure them, or control them. He simply asks that we hold their ropes long enough that they can

be in His presence and He can change them into what He wants them to be. He only asked Ananias to pray for Saul, not to evaluate his potential. If Ananias were to have asked Jesus, "What are you going to ask this ungodly man to do?" Jesus would have answered, "I am going to ask him to do the work I can't get you to do." ***And so, I set before the Napa Church the bottom line. We are to be a church where people from every walk of life can come and be in the presence of Jesus. They can know that we will hold their ropes without judging as long as they seek to know and grow in His likeness.***

That evening we met with nearly two hundred of the Napa Church members and their response indicated that we would have their full support in carrying out that mission. We have now been here for well over ten years and our message is still the same and their support in carrying out that message and ministry is still the same. Is everything perfect in Napa? No. Have there been challenges along the way? Yes. But, I can say without any question, this is the best match we have ever had in ministry.

Our first Sabbath as the pastoral couple leading the Napa Church was January 1, 2000. I thought that was a pretty remarkable starting date. Actually we started the night before, December 31, 1999 as we put together an Agape Feast and Communion Service to usher in a new beginning. That makes me the only pastor to have pastored this church in two millenniums.

As I began my message that first Sabbath I began with the words, "I didn't do it. I can't fix it. I don't want to hear about it. We're not looking back. We're moving forward." I was referring to the division and sparring that had taken place for the past several years that had caused many, many families to leave for other churches or to stop attending altogether. I wasn't interested or qualified to judge past grievances, but I wanted, instead, to enable the church to be open to a wide variety of needs, worship styles, and ministries, all the time keeping our eyes on Jesus.

Some of the programs that seem to be most effective here are focused on the church as a whole and many are focused on the youth. ***John Grys initiated the MARK (Monthly Acts of Random Kindness).***

Church members have passed out donuts and orange juice at the Post Office on April 15 for the past two years. They have given flowers to mothers around the neighborhood on Mother's Day and washed cars for free on Father's Day. They have offered a fifty-cent discount on gas at a nearby gas station while they washed windows and offered water. Each 4th of July they enter the local parade and pass out thousands of bottles of water from a truck that announces our church as offering the "Water of Life".

Pastor Sherilyn O"Ffill has redesigned our Pathfinder and Adventurer Clubs and through a high emphasis on reaching out to young families we have the front of the church full for Children's Story time and many baptisms from our Napa Christian Campus of Education, which became a full academy five years ago. Every year she conducts a "Baptismal Retreat" up at the conference camp and this has been a wonderful asset to our church growth.

When we arrived here the average attendance was just over 200. We haven't exactly exploded attendance, which now averages at 300, but you have to consider that I have, as of this writing, done 146 funerals in the past ten years. That is a lot of funerals to be sure and the majority have been people active in our church. With that said, I guess we have had moderate growth. What excites me most is the large number of young families that have come to the church. I have two fantastic associate pastors and my former Columbia Union President, Ron Wisbey, is now my Head Elder and it just doesn't get any better than that!

The work continues here in Napa, and surely there is a great deal more work that needs to be done and I know that I don't have all the gifts and resources to do it all. While the church has not seen significant number growth it has, I believe, experienced great spiritual growth. Certainly I can say, without argument, I, personally, have experienced great spiritual growth.

I hope and plan to stay in Napa for several more years. Only God knows what lies ahead as I approach the mid point of my seventh decade. I know that I want to stay in His service. I know that I want to continue to grow professionally and spiritually. I know that I am eternally grateful for all the blessings He has afforded me to this point and for the people who have held my ropes as I seek to stay in His presence. I know that my relationship with Christ is so much more than a list of proper Sabbath observances, or diet, or entertainment choices, or any other list of observable deeds. Any or all of these things can have an impact, but I know that we are all moved by different motivators and we all can respond with varying acts of worship.

I find that the older I get, the simpler my theology becomes. When I put the whole spiritual journey together it all comes down to my life at the foot of the cross. Just like my journey that initiated this book, I can wander through many different spiritual experiences in many different places, but there is nothing that can compare to coming home. The final exam has only one question on it: Do you believe that Jesus is the Son of God and have you asked Him to take all of your sins? Peter denied Christ three times and three times Jesus simply asked him to affirm his love and then bade him to go a minister to others. Paul said that he died daily. There is nothing like coming home!

Where do I go from here? Only God knows that and we are content to leave it all in His hands. Thirty seven years of ministry has been an amazing adventure, but we are always reminded that, "The best is yet to come!"

In the past five years I have lost both of my parents. I think the closing years of my relationship with my dad are worth sharing.

Through the years of ministry our relationship gradually warmed. Before that became reality, however, there was a time when I had a momentous awakening. My worst fear had always been becoming like my father and in years past I had indeed done that. The nagging fear continued to haunt me until one day, while we were pastoring in Montana, it was as if God spoke directly to me and said, "You can choose who your father is. I, too, am your Father." That realization changed my attitude toward my own dad and the relationship began to slowly heal.

As I began to see my parents really aging I made considerable effort to get up and see them as often as possible. We were living in Napa now and it was easier to either get a cheap flight or to drive up in one long day. Through subsequent visits the handshake between my father and I began to change. I could feel the touch lengthening and then I began placing my other hand on top of our grasped hands.

Oddly enough, it was Rolly who first said it. He said, “I guess it wouldn’t be such a terrible thing if a father gave his son a hug.” I can’t put into words what that meant to me, but it brings tears to my eyes as I write it just now. Love, affirmation, and a hug from your dad is precious at any age, even if you have to wait nearly sixty years to receive it. On subsequent visits there were more hugs and even those precious words, “I love you.” Past pains were forgotten and forgiven on both sides. Now, we were just father and son enjoying time together.

A little over five years ago I got a call from my sister telling me that Rolly was in the hospital and they suspected cancer. This was hardly a surprise as he smoked anywhere from ten to fifteen full sized cigars every day and inhaled every puff. I flew up immediately and it was obvious when I saw him in the hospital that this was going to be the final visit.

We talked with the doctors and they informed us that cancer was everywhere in his body. There were treatments that could prolong his life for a few weeks, or even months, but beyond that there was no hope. I, to some extent, took the lead and called the family together, which consisted only of mom, my sister and brother-in-law, myself and Rolly. We gathered around his hospital bed and I laid out before him exactly what his options were. I could see, immediately, the relief in his eyes when he realized that we were not going to work behind his back, but rather we chose to put the truth before him and let him make his own decision. He simply said that he wanted to go home.

We brought him home on Tuesday afternoon. He was so weak and frail. We placed him in his usual recliner in the living room and tried to make him comfortable. I am not ashamed to tell you that the next thing I did was to light his last cigar and hand it to him. He was too weak to finish it and just asked to be put in bed.

The doctor had prescribed liquid morphine and told me how to administer it. The plan was that we would wait until the weekend to give his brother and sisters and other family members a chance to come and say goodbye. Later that evening he called me into the bedroom and said, "I need to ask you a favor. I am hurting too bad. I can't wait 'til the weekend. You have the medication. Will you help me now?"

Again I asked all the family present to gather around his bed and we talked about his request and agreed that it should be his decision. Our daughter, Julie, was trying desperately to get up from the L.A. area in time to say goodbye to her only grandpa. We all agreed that I would start his liquid morphine that night.

A little later he called me into the room again and asked if I would help him onto the commode. I did that and afterward was cleaning him up. I saw an opportunity here and I wasn't going to miss it. I asked him, "Dad, (I wasn't about to call him Rolly now) when I was little did you ever change my diaper?" His response was, "No!" Actually his response included another word or two, but I'll leave them out here. "So," I asked, "Why in the world am I wiping you up now?" He got the most precious look on his face and said, "Oh…you got me!" I lovingly put him back to bed.

I then gave him the prescribed dosage the Dr. had told me to begin with. The Dr. had also said to feel comfortable in giving him as much as it takes to keep him comfortable. Rolly went to sleep then and two hours later I went in to give him his next dosage. He woke up with the most horrified look on his face and said, "What happened?" I told him that I was just giving him his next dosage of morphine. "How long does it take?" he asked. I told him the Dr. said it could take several days. The reaction I saw was one of absolute defeat. Then I made a decision and I told him, "Dad, I promise you that you will not have to wake up again." A look of peace and relief now came on his face and he said, "Thanks, Kid." Those were his last words and I cherish them.

I slept on the sofa that night and set my alarm for every hour and each hour I gave him another dosage of the precious pain reliever. We had been given eight bottles of liquid morphine. That was enough to last a full week or more. I never used a full half of one bottle. By three in the morning he was gone. Our daughter arrived at about seven. She was comforted by the fact that she had made multiple trips with me to see grandma and grandpa over the past two years and those memories were her solace.

I performed the memorial service that weekend and it was a privilege. It was also a great privilege to be able to be there with him for his entire last week. Words of love and affection were spoken and that was enough for a lifetime.

When I returned the seven unopened bottles of morphine to the pharmacy where they always shopped, the employees all came together and just wept. They had come to love this crusty old man with all their hearts. They also sent a large floral tribute to the service. It was the most unique I had ever seen. You see, my dad always ordered his cigars from them and he ordered them by the case. The arrangement they sent looked like it had cattails included, but in reality they were stalks with cigars on the end. I loved it and Rolly would have loved it even more.

Now, Mom was alone and we wondered how she would do. We had seen some signs of confusion for some time. My sister brought her down to Napa and they stayed with us for a short time and then Mom went home and got along by herself for a few months. Then we convinced her to try a local assisted living center and that worked out very well.

After a few months there she informed us that she had met someone and was quite "in love." This was definitely not in my plans for her future, but she was losing ground fast and she was so happy with her new friend. So, I flew up and we had a nice little "ceremony" in the fellowship room of the assisted living center. It wasn't a real wedding, but it made them both very happy and the whole community and staff enjoyed it very much.

Not too many months passed before Mom required more care and she had to be moved to another unit. She and her "friend" were still able to visit, but they never were really reunited. It was all downhill from there for my sweet, adorable, saintly mother. She was sent to Psych Wards and she only got more confused. Finally my sister placed her in a home that specialized in Alzheimer's and dementia and she actually did quite well there. I would visit and she always knew her "little boy" when he came.

Finally I got another call from my sister telling me that Mom was failing fast and that I had better come up. It couldn't have come at a worse time, but I won't go into those details here. I flew up and Mom was already in a coma. My sister and I just sat with her for the next two days and took turns sleeping. Both of us were there most of the time and one of us was always there.

Mom never spoke to us, but at one point very near the end we had the CD player going with some Bill Gaither music and suddenly she simply said, "Oh, I like that song!" We had never stopped talking to her because we knew that perhaps she could hear and absorb some of our words of love and comfort. This confirmed that.

Those were the only words we heard her speak. However, shortly before she died an amazing thing happened. The CD player was playing the simple song, "Jesus Loves Me." You know the tune. Mom, at times, would mumble sounds that made no sense, but suddenly it became clear that she was mumbling nonsensical sounds to the exact tune of "Jesus Loves Me." We believe those were her dying thoughts. Our Godly Mother was truly at peace with that assurance.

Now, my sister and I recognized that we were orphans! We also realized that we were now the older generation and we well knew what that meant! We drew great comfort in knowing that we had helped both parents pass on with dignity and surrounded by love. I am forever indebted to my sister and brother-in-law for the care that they gave to Mom during those last couple of years. I was in Napa and came as often as possible. They lived in the same town and cared for her and arranged for all of her appointments on a daily basis. Yes, it was a labor of love, but it was truly labor.

As I think of my precious mother and the things that she endured during her lifetime and how she held steadfastly to her faith in Jesus I am given great courage. I am also filled with enormous gratitude for her unquestioning love, encouragement, and, most of all, her prayers for me. Throughout my life she never, ever stopped praying for me and I know God heard each one of those prayers.

I'll never forget one conversation we had late in her life. She turned to me and said, "I am so thankful that neither of my children ever caused me any real pain." I knew right then and there that my mother had completely lost her mind. I began to "reason" with her by reminding her of my jail time as a child, my drinking years, my divorce, and other things that I'm not going to put on paper here. She just smiled and said, "Oh yes, there were those moments, but you never caused me any real hurt." God bless a mother's love! Rest sweetly, dear Mama. Jesus is coming soon!

By this point I have now slipped into my seventh decade. In fact I'm almost halfway through it. I have no idea what is coming next or when things might change. The body is not what it used to be as I turn 64, but I know that I have nothing to fear for the future except that I would forget God's leading in the past. I'll save the rest of the wrapping up for the next, and final, chapter.

Chapter the Last

What Did I Learn?

Endeavoring to bring this journey to completion, it has been just over a year since I hopped on the bike and rode into the sunrise. Well, I was heading east you know. I had the privilege (and it was indeed a privilege) to visit so many pastors and church leaders and to see so many places and approaches to worship that it is very challenging to even try to condense that into a summary.

Why has it taken so long? Well, there could be many "excuses" offered. The real truth is that it has just plain been a lot of work to put it into writing, have it edited, and rewritten. I got set back over the past month with a back surgery and some further complications that you don't need to be bothered with. I guess the biggest challenge has simply been the fact that I returned to pastor my church and it just takes a lot of time although they have been nothing but encouraging in the process.

I truly believe the good news is that the findings are still just as relevant as they were a year ago. I covered that aspect in the preface so let's just move on.

Just from a very personal point of view I renewed my love for and appreciation of this great country of ours with all of its divergent landscapes, weather, people groups, and personalities. Having lived outside of the U.S. for a number of years and having traveled through a significant portion of the world I can truly say that we live in a great country and that it is full of wonderful people. I learned that my backsides are as tough as I hoped they might be and that a good gel seat pad certainly helped me to be able to say that. I learned that I have an amazingly patient wife who loves me in spite of my abnormal dreams and aspirations. I was affirmed in my belief that my local church family loves me as well and that their prayers made a huge difference in my journey. I also learned that once I got back, finding the time to get this book written was not easy, but I think we're going to make it…finally!

As far as my dialogue with churches was concerned, let me start with what I found that encourages me. I found that, almost without exception, pastors were committed, dedicated, and working hard to make good things happen in their churches. They were trying to utilize both tried and true as well as new and creative ways to reach their communities. Most of them were optimistic and seemed to be fulfilled in their ministry.

I fully realize that, especially, the ones I did not know previously would be prone to make a positive presentation, but I sensed that they were genuine in what they shared with me. I heard about an amazingly wide range of ideas designed to attract new interests and build relationships in the community. We have seen prayer rooms intending to draw visitors. We have seen community outreach centers meeting significant needs and drawing strong support from area businesses. I saw car shows, state of the art media, health programs, home makeovers, and amazing dramatizations of Bethlehem used to catch the minds and hearts of a nation living in fast changing and troubling times. I also saw a great deal of traditional evangelism, seminars, and Bible study programs aimed at those who are already tuned in to things of a spiritual nature.

So, what is the best approach? What is really working? What I saw was that in the vast majority of churches we are just hanging on and not really growing. In almost every church the book membership is significantly over the active membership, often nearly double. My general observation in all of this is that we need to do a better job of engaging people both inside and outside of the church. Let me explain.

Looking back on my visits on Sabbath mornings I was surprised and disappointed to find that I was, for the most part, too often ignored as I entered and wandered about. I did not go up and introduce myself to people, nor did I try to avoid being greeted. I simply walked in and walked around to see what might happen. In one contemporary church I entered the foyer, looked around and found a bulletin, found a rest room, entered the sanctuary, went back into the foyer and finally went back into the sanctuary and sat down without having a word said. During the "meet and greet" time a couple greeted me. After the service was over I walked and stood in the foyer again for more than ten minutes without contact and I left.

On one Sabbath I was taken to church by friends and introduced, so that doesn't count. Out of the other five Sabbaths I was only really greeted and included one time. That was the New Creation Fellowship near Lincoln, Nebraska. That time made up for all the others. I was greeted, hugged, given a bulletin and a study guide, led to a refreshment table, introduced to a class, and invited to dinner after church. Out of my Sabbath experiences I know which church I would seek to be a part of. The church in Aldergrove, B.C. also was very warm and has a very attractive bounty of activities to draw young families.

It is so easy to enjoy the warm fellowship of friends on Sabbath morning and get involved in conversation that we miss the mission and the opportunities that God gives us to make a first impression on those who may be seeking a place of worship. Welcoming them from the pulpit does not get the job done.

It must have been very obvious that I was a visitor in every church I attended as I wore my motorcycle clothing consisting of specialized jeans with stretch fabric where stretching material is most needed, a chain to keep my wallet attached, and leather jacket. Maybe they were afraid to engage me, but I don't really think I looked that fearsome, just different. We must be bold in reaching out to those we do not know.

In larger churches we have to be willing to risk introducing ourselves and asking the name of people who may have been attending that church for twenty years. If God has called you to be a missionary to your home church you need to overtly greet and welcome every person you don't know. The one you miss may be the one God sent.

We also need to do a better job of engaging people outside the church walls. The most effective means of witnessing is simply talking to people. I could write an entire separate book just about the blessings of engaging people in conversation. I'll just include a couple of examples.

I was standing in the arrival area of San Francisco International Airport waiting for family to arrive from Germany. I always love to watch people and I especially enjoy doing so at airports. I couldn't help but notice a young man standing behind a pillar and holding a bouquet of flowers. I watched him for a while and finally I approached him and said, "Let me guess. You're not waiting for your dad."

"No," he said, "I'm waiting for my fiancé from Spain."

"Aha," I replied, "are you getting married soon?"

"Yes, we're getting married next month," was his response.

"And do you have a preacher?" I queried.

He informed me that they were just going to go to the courthouse, as they didn't have any money for a minister and a real wedding.

That's when I said, "Well, I'm a preacher and I absolutely love to do weddings, and I wouldn't charge you a cent."

Then he told me that the problem was that he was from out of town and was stationed at Travis Air Force Base in Fairfield.

That's when I told him that I also lived in Fairfield.

Long story short: I performed their wedding in their home and we are still in touch with each other several years later.

On another occasion I was flying home to California from Washington, D.C. and the flight was going to be very full. I was seated in an aisle seat and the window seat was already occupied and I waited to see who was going to have the middle seat.

I watched as people continued to board and I confess to silently praying, "Lord, not that one. No, not that one either." Then I saw a woman with red hair tied into a ponytail. She was wearing a sleeveless blouse, jeans, and a leather vest, and I thought, "OK, Lord, I could probably talk about motorcycles with that one." Yes, she sat there.

We said hello to each other and just made small talk. I did ask her if she rode and she confirmed that she did. I guessed her to be in her mid 50's and she looked quite strong with tattooed arms, which I thought fit with the biker picture.

After we were well into the flight we began to talk a bit and I asked her about her trip. She told me that she was on her way home after some meetings related to a charity she was involved in. I asked her what kind of work she did and she informed me that she was a blacksmith. Now, there's something you don't hear from a woman too often. Now I was interested and I asked a few more questions and showed that I was ready to listen to her story.

She had begun working as a regular blacksmith and specialized in making horseshoes. But, she had the ability to simply tell by looking as to how the shoe should be shaped and had an artistic gift to make it a perfect fit. She went on to tell me how she met a man who was prominent in his artistic wrought iron work. He taught others, but would only take on six students at any time. She told me that she began to pray that God would open a door for her and that her prayers were answered in a manner that she considered to be God's direct leading.

I, obviously, was very interested in her expressions of faith, but I never said a word about my work or my faith. I was just listening. She then pulled out a portfolio showing some of her work and I was blown away. This lady specialized in doors, windows, and artwork for homes in Carmel, Pebble Beach, and other upscale localities. She showed me a door that cost $250,000. I didn't order one! She kept talking about the Spiritual Gift that God had given her and His leading and guiding in her life. Then she volunteered that she wasn't actively involved in any particular church. She said, "If I were to join an actual church, I would probably join the Seventh-day Adventist Church." I just started smiling.

She asked me what was so funny and I told her then that I was the Pastor of the Napa Community Seventh-day Adventist Church. That was when she started laughing. She and her husband, who was head of the chemistry department at UC Davis, live well out into the country east of Sacramento. Several months later I called her and asked if our motorcycle group from the church could ride out to her place and see some of her work. The date was set and twenty-six bikes rolled down her drive and she and her husband had prepared dinner and dessert for all of us and we got a grand demonstration of her God given talents.

I can't tell you that either of these contacts joined the church, but I can tell you that they have a very positive attitude toward our church. What God does with the seed is His business. I just want to be available to sew them wherever He directs.

I have found consistently that when I talk to people and engage them in airports, airplanes, grocery checkout lines, on the golf course, (I've done two weddings from contacts made with strangers on the golf course by simply asking them if they have a preacher when I learn they are planning on marriage) or anywhere else I am with people. You don't even have to be a gifted conversationalist. Just be a good listener and ask God to tell you what to say when an opening occurs. We must engage people. We need to make friends with them on their turf and warmly include them when they come on ours.

I was pleased to find that almost all of the churches I visited were making an effort to keep their buildings and their grounds attractive and that is so important. Equally important is making sure our places of worship are easy to find. I must say that I did spend a significant amount of time trying to locate some churches. Highway signs are helpful and signs on the property are equally important. In a handful of cases I really wondered if they were deliberately trying to hide.

Looking back on my contact with seventy churches I don't believe the real key lies in the style of worship. I believe you can be contemporary or traditional and still have a vibrantly growing church. The secret is in loving people into your fellowship. We need all styles of worship. We certainly need to stop judging and putting down any style that is not our preference. The criticism seems to go equally in both directions and it is all contrary to the calling that Christ has given to us.

The church will continue to debate theological issues, standards, and worship styles until Jesus comes, but if we will simply focus on bringing people into a saving relationship with Christ I believe He will come more quickly.

Allow me to touch on one more issue that I feel is holding back church growth. I came back feeling that far too many pastors were working with their hands tied. Many of the churches, particularly long established churches, are not willing to allow the pastor to lead. Too often the local

leadership feels ownership of the church. In a broad sense that is a good thing. They need to be actively involved in "their" church, but not to the extent that they won't allow God to bring them a leader and allow him or her to lead.

I believe one great contributing factor to this is the reality that pastors have moved or been moved too frequently. How is a church supposed to fully get behind a pastor and support their creativity only to find that in three to five years down the road that pastor is gone and they have to adjust to a whole different set of gifts and ideas?

Churches also get comfortable in what they currently have and are often unwilling to surrender that comfort to "creativity." I shouldn't have to point out that our world and our families are changing dramatically every generation. We don't have to leave and abandon the things that are meaningful to the older generations, but we must be willing to tweak formats, images, methods, and even music, to help our young adults feel like there is a place for them too.

To complicate the issue I am convinced that too many conference leaders do not do enough to encourage creativity. Conference financial support and re-election comes largely from the older and traditional sectors of the membership and administration is often reluctant to support new options that older members may view as worldly, feeling that it encourages a lowering of standards.

Frustration is high among many of the pastors and church members I visited also because I believe that far too often pastoral vacancies are simply "filled" rather than working to truly match gifts with needs. I can't put all the blame for this on conference leadership. Many times their choices are limited and they are doing the best they can with talent and funds that they have at their disposal. I have seen, however, in some conferences where there is an individual who works closely with administration, but is somewhat distanced from it, and is given the primary responsibility of overseeing pastoral placement and pastoral satisfaction, that things work better.

In our time of fiscal challenges and downsizing of conference personnel most conferences have given up the separate designation of a Ministerial Director. Even in those conferences that do maintain that position the director usually does not have a significant role in pastoral assignment and also has to carry enough other responsibilities that they cannot focus on pastoral health.

If we believe that the local church is truly the driving force of our denomination and if we believe that God calls and equips men and women to lead those churches then I think we can do more to empower the local church and church pastors. We must also find ways to allow the local churches to have funding for new and creative ways of making connection with the community.

Now, I have been back in my own church, my beloved Napa Community SDA Church and I feel so blessed and privileged to be connected with this church family. I am blessed with two associates that I admire and love for each of their distinctive gifts. I am blessed with local church leadership that truly leads and contributes incredible numbers of hours to make things happen.

I am faced with the challenges and shortcomings and failures that are unique to my own application of the things I have seen and learned from this journey, but also I give glory to God for the equally unique ministerial gifts that He has placed in this earthen vessel that has allowed us to become the church we are today.

I am still learning and growing after nearly thirty-seven years of ministry. I hope I never stop until Jesus comes. ***I reaffirm that I am a Seventh-day Adventist Christian and that I love this church. I acknowledge that this church belongs to God and that I am only a humble servant and steward. I am not called or qualified to grapple with doctrinal wording, or to oversee the behavior of individuals or the teaching of every pastor and professor. I have been called to share the everlasting gospel to a world that desperately needs to hear it.***

We need gifted leaders to administrate the "business" of the church and to orchestrate policies. I truly value and appreciate those that have been called to that, mostly, thankless task. We have been given a means of allowing the church body as a whole to have input into the orchestration of that business. ***My plea would be that all of us would accept that our first calling is to share the love of Christ and build relationships with people. To those who spend so much time writing and***

wrangling over what somebody else is doing or teaching, rather than simply expressing a concern to the proper people in a proper way and trusting God to direct those He has placed in power, I would ask, "When is the last time you personally reached out and led someone to the foot of the cross and witnessed the redemption of a soul?"

When the church is fundamentally about our Father's business, then the Son of God will appear with healing in His wings. May the day be soon!

Allow me to close with a few paragraphs from the book, "Acts of the Apostles" by Ellen White, in the Chapter entitled, "A Faithful Witness"

"After the descent of the Holy Spirit, when the disciples went forth to proclaim a living Saviour, their one desire was the salvation of souls. They rejoiced in the sweetness of communion with saints. They were tender, thoughtful, self-denying, willing to make any sacrifice for the truth's sake. In their daily association with one another, they revealed the love that Christ had enjoined upon them. By unselfish words and deeds they strove to kindle this love in other hearts.

"Such a love the believers were ever to cherish. They were to go forward in willing obedience to the new commandment. So closely were they to be united with Christ that they would be enabled to fulfill all His requirements. Their lives were to magnify the power of a Saviour who could justify them by His righteousness.

"But gradually a change came. The believers began to look for defects in others. Dwelling upon mistakes, giving place to unkind criticism, they lost sight of the Saviour and His love. They became more strict in regard to outward ceremonies, more particular about the theory than the practice of the faith. In their zeal to condemn others, they overlooked their own errors. They lost the brotherly love that Christ had enjoined, and, saddest of all, they were unconscious of their loss. They did not realize that happiness and joy were going out of their lives and that, having shut the love of God out of their hearts, they would soon walk in darkness." AA, 547, 548

Are we in danger of mirroring those words today? Is it that spirit of self-importance that is in any way holding back the preaching of the gospel to a dying world so that Jesus can return? You will have to look into your own heart and prayerfully search for the answer my friend. My prayer is that we will all be willing to do just that and surrender our will, our thoughts, our preferences, and yes, even our personal doctrinal understandings to Jesus. That doesn't mean we have to toss them aside. It does mean that we have to stop squabbling over them incessantly while lost souls are passing us by on either side.

We are a called church…a chosen people. We have a message of hope. We have a message of a merciful Father who gave His Son that we might have everlasting life. We have an everlasting gospel to share. Let us be about the Father's business for He is not willing that any should perish, but that all should have everlasting life!

There you have it, my friends. What a journey it has been. When I say that I mean the journey around the U.S. and my own personal spiritual journey. May God continue to lead and guide and reform me, and may He do the same for His church.

Thanks for riding along and for listening to my personal testimony as well. Let us pray for each other and determine to meet together not by the riverside, not by the tree of life, but let's meet together at the feet of Jesus. That is the one place where we are all truly equal.

About the Author

For the past eleven years Marvin Wray has been the Lead Pastor at the Napa Community SDA Church in Napa, California. Previously he has served churches in several other locations, including six years in Hong Kong and five years as the Ministerial Director for the Potomac Conference of Seventh-day Adventists in Virginia, Washington, D.C., and southern Maryland.

He has previously co-authored two other books with Len McMillian. In 1994 they wrote, "First-Class Male" and in 1996 they followed with, "Putting Up With Mr. Right." Marvin has been a frequent speaker for men's retreats, pastor's retreats, couple's retreats, campmeetings, and other convocations both in the U.S. as well as Asia and Europe.

He has been married to his wife, Ingrid, for almost forty years and they have three married children and five perfect grandchildren. Both Marvin and Ingrid love to travel, walk, browse through small out of the way towns and just be together. They have a perfect marriage in that Ingrid loves to golf and ride the motorcycle and Marvin loves to go shopping with her.

His real passion in ministry is to share the absolute assurance of God's gift of salvation and to make that as simple as possible. Building real relationships with other people and with Jesus Christ is the fundamental structure of a Christian journey and that journey will never end throughout all of eternity.

Fun loving, humorous, dedicated, and just a little off the wall are words and expressions that are often used to describe this author.

CPSIA information can be obtained at www.ICGtesting.com
Printed in the USA
LVOW060817230212

269974LV00003B/2/P

9 781452 099712